# HELPING BUSINESS— THE LIBRARY'S ROLE IN COMMUNITY ECONOMIC DEVELOPMENT

## A How-To-Do-It Manual

Maxine Bleiweis

*HOW-TO-DO-IT MANUALS FOR LIBRARIANS*

*NUMBER 73*

NEAL-SCHUMAN PUBLISHERS, INC.
New York, London

Published by Neal-Schuman Publishers, Inc.
100 Varick Street
New York, NY 10013

Copyright © 1997 by Maxine Bleiweis

Printed and bound in the United States of America.

**Library of Congress Cataloging-in-Publication Data**

Bleiweis, Maxine.
    Helping business : the library's role in community economic
development : a how-to-do-it manual / Maxine Bleiweis.
        p.    cm.—(How-to-do-it manuals for librarians ; 73)
    Includes bibliographical references and index.
    ISBN 1-55570-231-7
    1. Public libraries—Services to business and industry—United
States.  I. Title.  II. Series: How-to-do-it manuals for libraries ;
no. 73.
Z675.B8B58    1997
027.6'9—dc21                                                              97-5291

55.00

# CONTENTS

# FIGURES

# FOREWORD

Many public officials and citizens rely on traditional municipal contacts for economic development information. During the past decade, municipal libraries have strived to fill an "informational vacuum" in the municipal marketplace for valuable economic development services. More importantly, many community libraries now provide computer training, job-search workshops, and access to regional and state-wide job banks. Gone are the "ivory tower" days for local libraries. Our local community libraries still contain their share of books, but the wealth of new periodicals and reference materials that relate to economic development have increased dramatically.

In recent years, our public libraries have become a valuable resource to business leaders, small business persons, budding entrepreneurs, as well as job-seekers. Many library directors have tailored their services to fit the unique needs of their community. As libraries adapt to the evolving needs of their respective communities, new computer hardware and software applications, coupled with the wealth of information available from new databases and the Internet, have helped to bridge the gap between the public and private sectors.

The astute municipal chief executive officer, working with their library director, needs to promote the resources available from their public library to the business sector. You can find out about zoning matters from the planning department, and the availability of utilities from the public works experts, but you can only check your markets, the latest trends in your field, and leading-edge periodicals to promote your business, from your community's library.

Maxine Bleiweis's book, *Helping Business: The Library's Role in Community Economic Development*, brings together, for the first time, many of the ways our local libraries are improving their services to the private sector to promote economic growth. The information and resources available from libraries makes them valuable partners in stimulating the local economy. This book takes a giant step in the right direction by codifying the available information about the many ways that libraries can enhance their role in this regard.

As a practicing city manager for many years, I would wholeheartedly recommend this book to other municipal officials, library directors, and private sector executives, in their quest for information about new ways to promote economic development within their community.

Roger L. Kemp, Ph.D.
City Manager
Meriden, CT

# PREFACE

Public libraries are often a vastly underused business resource. You can change that, though, by aggressively pursuing businesses in your town until they naturally turn to you for their information needs. *Helping Business—The Library's Role in Community Economic Development* teaches librarians how to identify the information needs of businesses, respond to those needs through improvements in the way information is made available, and then to actively market its library services in the business community. This book's organization parallels a step-by-step process for achieving this transformation.

The first chapter provides an introduction to economic development and the initial planning for serving the business community or enhancing existing services. It outlines the shift in thinking that libraries must undergo, shows that businesses need information at different stages, and facilitates your rethinking of your library's role in the community.

Chapter Two discusses the steps libraries can take to reach out and get in touch with the information needs of the business community through such means as using focus groups, surveys and questionnaires, business audits, partnerships with the chamber of commerce, and working with the town planning and zoning commission and town/school/business collaboratives.

After looking outward to assess the needs of the community, the next step is to look inward to evaluate the resources you have and see where improvements can be made. Chapter Three explains how to assess the value of the library personnel, equipment, collection materials, and even the building itself with regards to the types of services you can offer to business. It is not enough to have the adequate collections, electronic information, etc. if your staff lacks the skills necessary to conduct the proper research, navigate the Net, or promote these skills to the community. Chapter Four addresses training staff to sharpen these skills, familiarizing them with commonly used business terms, and hiring advisors with business experience.

Once the library is prepared to fulfill the needs of the business community, the next step is to ensure a steady stream of patrons interested in making use of your new and expanded offerings. Very often the library can be ignored as an information resource if businesses are not in the habit of utilizing its services. Simply getting your foot in the door of a local corporation can go a long way in ensuring that your library will be trusted as a resource and looked to for guidance. Chapter Five explains how librarians can break into the circle of leading business minds in town and identify an advocate—someone who will champion your cause. Library staff can also network with leaders at trade shows, community boards, or commissions or conferences.

Chapter Six describes a collection of practical ideas such as compiling a town business directory, producing a business newsletter, providing community information packets for relocated employees, offering business counseling or tax assistance, and having a notary public on staff.

Chapter Seven covers several marketing approaches libraries can use to make themselves a more visible presence in the business community. These include utilizing the local newspaper, radio, Internet newsgroups, direct mail campaigns, programming, and advertising.

Finally, *Helping Business* discusses how to gauge results of your efforts, from recognition and personal satisfaction to increased funding. Appendixes cover how to write a business plan for entrepreneurs, organizing focus groups at a reasonable cost, and a glossary of much-used business terms with which staff members should familiarize themselves. "Guidelines for Medical, Legal, and Business Responses at General Reference Desks," a thorough bibliography and index, and the strategic plan for a regional library round out these resources.

Regardless of the size and nature of your local businesses, *Helping Business* will lead you through the step-by-step processes in order for your library to become a valuable economic development asset.

# ACKNOWLEDGMENTS

Throughout the country, librarians and libraries are linking up with their business communities. I first became aware of the importance of economic development to librarians with the formation of an Economic Vitality Taskforce of the Connecticut Library Association. Susan Bullock, the original founder of the taskforce, is to be commended for her foresight in teaching others about its importance. I also thank the following for sharing their experiences: the public libraries of Southfield, Michigan; Rolling Meadows, Illinois; Iowa City, Iowa; Cedar Falls, Iowa; Union County, Florida; Savanna, Illinois; Canton, Illinois; Fort Wayne, Indiana; Pekin, Illinois; London, Ontario, Canada; Lincoln, Illinois; Meriden, Connecticut; Gwinnett-Forsyth County, Georgia; Glendale, Arizona; Johnson County, Kansas; Carroll County, Maryland; Milwaukee, Wisconsin; and Bellevue, Iowa.

Business librarians from United Technologies, Aetna Life & Casualty, and Loctite Corporation gave me insight into the corporate library world. The Illinois Institute for Rural Affairs, the Business/Industry Affairs Department of Littleton, Colorado, and the Morrison Institute for Public Policy at the School of Public Affairs of Arizona State University freely shared their findings and studies. One particularly successful venture has been spearheaded by the Illinois State Library under the direction of Bridgett Lamont. Throughout this book, the reader will find examples from this program of partnerships between libraries and local Chambers of Commerce.

Closer to home, I thank Newington, Connecticut's, Town Manager Keith Chapman who listened carefully to the possible role of the public library in economic development, implemented it, and went on to champion it in other communities. Small business owners Diane Lewis and Olga Fernandez took the time to reflect on the value of the library to their respective businesses and to act as emissaries for library publicity. Fellow town department head Roy Zartarian's writing expertise and appreciation and understanding of library business services greatly contributed to the completion of this volume.

And, most importantly, I acknowledge the work of Shirlee-Ann Kober, business librarian at the Newington Library. Due to her expertise and willingness to forge ahead, the library's role in economic development has been successful in the community and has been able to develop as a model to be used in other communities.

Of course, all of the above people were invaluable, but, ultimately, the responsibility for every word in this book is mine.

# INTRODUCTION

What do all these scenarios have in common?

*The local manager of a computer operations center receives the authority from the central office to hire personnel, but first she needs some sample job descriptions, competitive salary ranges, and typical benefits offered for the position.*

*A home-based business person offering secretarial services to small companies wants to produce a newsletter promoting the service. He would also like to identify specifically potential customers in the health-care field.*

*The owner of a small but active hair salon hears there's a faster way to make "zulu" knots—a new craze in hair fashion.*

*A middle-aged marketing vice president, facing unemployment because of a corporate restructuring, wants to investigate sources of venture capital.*

These are all actual scenarios that have been presented to reference staff at local public libraries. They typify the business community's growing recognition and utilization of library resources. Simply by responding to such questions, public librarians have become participants in their local economic development programs.

Throughout the country, municipalities have recognized the value to their residents of a strong business base. Government support for business generally takes the form of tax incentives, zoning adjustments, and job training programs. Yet the public library can add a vigorous and vital dimension to these traditional approaches.

What gives libraries the edge in becoming such an important economic development asset? Information. Business today is driven by it. And providing timely, accurate, relevant information—a commodity essential to business growth—is the function of the public library. People making sound business decisions fuel the economy by enabling the growth of prosperous communities and individuals.

But there may be something standing in the way of a library's greater involvement in economic development initiatives: a limited perception of the library's abilities, especially on the part of the library itself. Libraries, except those large enough to operate a specialized business department, have customarily limited the "business of business" to the purchase of such materials as standard directories and "how to" books and tapes. The reference staff is often relieved when a business person asks only, "Do you have *Standard and Poor's?*" Since they bring to the profession a liberal arts background, many public librarians cannot fluently speak the language of business. The absence of such a capability may be one of the leading reasons that libraries confine their role in the business environment to that of a custodian of specialized publications.

There is also a practical aspect to the involvement of public libraries in economic development. Libraries are dependent upon a tax base supported in large part by business, and should therefore have a vested interest in the support of that tax base. Literate communities are more apt than illiterate ones to use and support libraries. A community with a strong tax base is more inclined than others to adequately support its library. Without customers, libraries will not exist. Therefore, we need to be involved in literacy training both in terms of actual reading and of developing knowledge bases. Now turn that around to money instead of customers. Without funding, libraries will not exist. The tax base upon which they depend has to be able to fund them. Therefore, we have a vested interest in keeping that tax base vibrant.

A political aspect is even more compelling. The community leaders who make decisions regarding support for municipal budgets are often business people. The better they understand how the library is in part responsible for the success of local business and overall economic growth, the more likely it is that funds will be appropriated for operations. While service to children and their families is critical, it doesn't have the same (economic) impact as when a business owner can say, "I owe much of the success of my company's latest decision to the information I received from the public library."

Whatever a library's size, it can take a leading role in providing information to businesses and becoming a principal player on an economic development team. Many libraries already possess the foundation in terms of their staff and collection. This book will explore that foundation as well as the tools, materials, and designs to build from it for the benefit of both the community and the library itself.

# 1

# GETTING READY TO SERVE THE BUSINESS COMMUNITY

## WHAT IS ECONOMIC DEVELOPMENT, AND WHAT DOES IT HAVE TO DO WITH LIBRARIES?

Simply put, economic development is the growth of business in a variety of ways. It can include activities to create wealth, generate rising real incomes, and increase employment. Without even realizing it, libraries have participated in these activities for decades with little fanfare.

But now the economic development picture is changing. Communities used to do what was commonly termed "smokestack chasing" (pursuing manufacturing businesses interested in relocation), creating an infrastructure of highways, water and sewer lines, and telecommunications to meet businesses' needs. Planners could sit back, satisfied that a great catch had been landed and harvested in terms of tax dollars. Now the emphasis is, and needs to be, placed on retaining existing businesses and equipping those businesses to compete in a global economy.

A global economy means that wages paid and other costs accrued in the United States are compared to those in other countries. Domestic companies cannot compete on a cost basis when work such as assembly or data entry can be done more cheaply. Instead, our competitive edge needs to stem from innovation, advancements, and knowledge-intensive products and services. Once, low cost and high volume used to be the keys to success. Today the keys are quality, innovation, and responsiveness to change.

In a 1990 keynote speech, David Osborne put forth that "economic development is not about recruiting plants. It's not about doing deals. It's about changing cultures, changing institutions, and changing markets to make them work better in the radically new economic environment we find ourselves in today. And information is the most important tool we have with which to make those changes."[1] Providing information is a primary mission of the public library.

The Corporation for Enterprise Development, an economic development support agency, has identified "new rules" that it urges the United States to play by in the 1990s.[2] Three rules are especially relevant to library services.

## RULE: "COMPETITIVE BUSINESSES ARE ATTRACTED TO AND GROW IN THE HIGHEST VALUE LOCATIONS, NOT THE CHEAPEST."

This represents a shift in thinking about business location. Businesses are rethinking the advisability of moving a plant from the high-cost Northeast to the low-cost South as a way to cut costs. In a recent letter to the editor in the *Hartford Courant*, a former resident of an affluent Hartford suburb warned others who might be considering emulating her family's journey south with the relocation of their employer. She cited the difference in standards in park and recreation facilities, the dearth of cultural offerings, and, most of all, the paltry library resources for her preschooler as well as for herself. She urged people to examine what made them value their time at work and play and think twice before accepting anything less than what they've become accustomed to.[3]

An employer's most critical asset is its workforce. If the support structure in the relocation community cannot meet the experienced worker's self-development and cultural needs, the employer may have to cultivate labor that is already in the area and spend valuable time bringing workers up to speed. The town of Southfield, Michigan, has produced an advertisement for national magazines that clearly recognizes this problem and goes so far as to mention the library (Figure 1–1). Quality library service benefits both the relocated and the local new worker.

## RULE: "ECONOMIC DEVELOPMENT, LIKE CHARITY, BEGINS AT HOME."

Many communities are making efforts at economic development by establishing research and development centers, technology transfer systems, venture capital resources, and new education reform measures. Libraries, if situated in the right place, can capitalize on those efforts and show how they partner any effort to enhance the local economy and retrain a workforce.

In a knowledge-based economy, educated and skilled people provide the principal competitive edge. These people are not simply reporting to work each day and doing what is laid out for them. Instead they are asking why, questioning procedures, and developing new methods. Change requires information that libraries can supply. And having information available and getting it to those who need it are the challenges librarians face.

**FIGURE 1–1   Advertisement for Southfield, Michigan**

# 成 功

# Erfolg
# Succés
# Successo
# Ycnéx
# Prosperar

*In any language, Southfield, Michigan translates into Success.*

The world of commerce takes anchor in Southfield, home to one hundred and forty Fortune 500 companies and 46 foreign firms—more than any community in Oakland County. It's easy to see why so many international businesses make Southfield their home. Abundant, prestigious office space at great rates, given our nearly 60 office buildings with more than 100,000 square feet. Superb freeway and highway access to all areas of metropolitan Detroit. A sense of community—with excellent city services, including our business-oriented library; attractive shopping and dining; and inviting neighborhoods and parks.

For more information contact Southfield Community Development at (810) 354-48483.

**SOUTHFIELD.** THE CENTER OF IT ALL.

**RULE: "GOVERNMENT IS AN ESSENTIAL PARTNER WITH THE PRIVATE SECTOR IN MAKING THE STRATEGIC INVESTMENTS IN PEOPLE, INSTITUTIONS AND INFRASTRUCTURE THAT GLOBALLY COMPETITIVE FIRMS REQUIRE."**

The city of Littleton, Colorado, has established a town department devoted to assisting the 1,600 businesses in the town. The department follows a three-pronged approach, but the centerpiece is what is termed "World Class Research." Essentially, the Economic Development Department of Littleton provides the services of a librarian and computerized database searching as a benefit of being a Littleton business. The municipal government realizes the value of partnering with business people to bring about success.

## CHANGING YOUR LIBRARY'S ROLE

The Morrison Institute for Public Policy at the School of Public Affairs at Arizona State University conducted extensive research on the use of libraries by the Arizona business community in 1990 (Figure 1–2). The findings showed that only about 2 percent of the businesses polled mentioned libraries as a main source of business-related information, and that personal contacts were the most relied-upon resources.

The Institute's studies also showed that businesses less than five years old were more likely to use a public library than were older businesses. This finding fits with the testimony of the owner of a small public relations firm, who described her own information-seeking progression as her business developed:

1. The Entrepreneurial Stage: when options are being explored and the business defined; information is needed at this stage in depth and in quantity.

2. The Repetition Stage: when the business is up and running and the business person is doing what he or she does well; little further information is needed at this stage.

3. The "Grow or Die" Stage: when competition offers the same product or service better and cheaper, or when the business owner feels the need to grow in more directions; the need for information now is as high as in the first phase.

The town of Littleton calls such businesses "gazelles"—small, fast-growing companies creating new products. These enterprises

## FIGURE 1-2 Main Sources of Information for Small Businesses (initial responses)

| Principal Source | % |
|---|---|
| 1. Personal* | 46.2 |
| 2. Magazines | 36.0 |
| 3. Newspapers | 12.8 |
| 4. Manufacturers/suppliers | 12.5 |
| 5. Organizations/associations | 8.6 |
| 6. Directories | 8.2 |
| 7. Neutral** | 7.8 |
| 8. Schools/Seminars | 4.4 |
| 9. Government | 4.1 |
| 10. Miscellaneous | 3.8 |
| 11. Business consultants | 3.2 |
| 12. Trade shows and conventions | 2.4 |
| **13. Libraries** | **2.3** |
| 14. Broadcast Media | 1.9 |
| 15. Advertising | 1.6 |
| 16. Computer databases | 1.0 |
| 17. Financial institutions | 0.3 |

*Specific responses included: personal business, business colleagues, employees, friends and relatives, clients and customers, personal contacts, word of mouth, mail, flyers, junk mail, and previous owners.
**Indicates a response such as "nothing," "don't know," or "not sure."

Source: Statewide Small Business Study, Morrison Institute for Public Policy, School of Public Affairs, ASU, July 1990.

represent the middle ground between the "mom and pop" operations, which often do not expand, and the large companies that are presently reengineering. Because of their information requirements, gazelles are the businesses with which libraries can establish the most satisfactory partnership efforts.

Businesses use information as a tool to make changes. Libraries contain that information, but they need to let businesses know that. Those involved in economic development design strategies for building a strong business community that supports innovation, entrepreneurship, and cooperation between the public and private sectors. Librarians can be leaders in planning and executing such strategies (Figure 1-3).

**FIGURE 1-3    Information Available at Local Public Libraries**

**Where would you go to get information regarding . . .**

1.   the number of companies headquartered in Connecticut?

2.   manufacturers of rubber stamps in Western Europe?

3.   a list of questions that cannot be asked on job applications?

4.   the location of Sentry Bank on Cape Cod, Massachusetts?

5.   the address for dental labs in Minnesota?

6.   information on mentorship programs between schools and businesses?

7.   the pros and cons of auto leasing?

8.   companies in Connecticut employing between 500 and 1,000 people?

9.   names, addresses, and telephone numbers for pharmacies in zip code areas beginning with 184 and 285?

10.  examples of sales letters?

11.  nonpublic metal fabricators in New York with sales between $15 and $25 million?

12.  addresses of trade publications?

13.  evaluations of fax machines?

14.  existing inventions for automatic opening doors?

15.  market research studies on biodegradable plastics?

**The answer: Your local public library!**

Source: Questions were actual queries at the public library in Newington, Connecticut.

Many librarians have been intrigued by the possibilities of getting involved with the business community but hold back for a variety of reasons. Primary among these is *fear of failure*, but this is possibly the most unfounded reason. As you read on, you will find that business questions are similar to those you already process without a formalized economic development effort. Questions symptomatic of the fear of failure might be:

- What if I don't understand the terms the business person uses?
- Won't I look foolish?
- What if we don't have the resources to answer the questions?

- What if our designated business librarian is on vacation? Who'll take care of it?
- How can we possibly take on one more thing?
- What if we raise expectations we can't meet?

Another stumbling block is a hesitation to take *risks*. The foray into serving the business community for the first time definitely entails risks—as well as retraining, rethinking, and planning. Convincing people who range from staff to library board members to government officials to the business people themselves that you have a vital role in the economic development of your community and then *proving* it requires the willingness to take a risk. The stakes seem higher because there's real profit and loss potential. We're not talking about supplying information for a paper that will be graded in an academic world. No; *you* are trying to sell a concept and a service, so you're obligated to deliver. There is a subtle difference between dealing with a patron who will go elsewhere if you cannot satisfy the need, and the business person whom you have been cultivating who presents a "let's see if the library can really help me" attitude.

The need to *retrain* can also inhibit reaching out to the business world. Serving the business community is not simply a matter of buying a good collection and putting out an "open for business" sign. It means getting out of the library and speaking directly to the business person. Presently, reference librarians are, by and large, providing reactive services. Serving the business community well means training and educating a new consumer market. It means marketing the library's services, constantly promoting what can be done, and doing it. It requires networking, learning new terms, and coming to grips with the fact that we need to serve a unique population differently. This population does not fit the mold. To serve the business community effectively, librarians need to become comfortable with networking, learning a new terminology, and departing from the traditional forms of service.

Essentially, it all boils down to *rethinking* one's role. The librarian has been traditionally more of a reactor and guide, showing someone how to find the answer to a question at the library. Service to business people is different. There can be no expectation that the business person should have to use indexes, catalogs, etc.; they should simply be able to ask the question and digest the answer. This new category of patron requires a different concept of service delivery along with the necessary operational changes.

A final facet to bear in mind is *timing*. One librarian of a small community mentioned that she would not have gotten involved in economic development if she had not felt that her library was doing the "basics" well first. To her, that meant that circulation was about as high as it could go, that all children were accommodated through storytelling, that people were happy with the popular reading collection and basic reference services, and that the staff performed at a very high level.

You might choose not to wait to achieve those kinds of goals before considering service to businesses. But it does follow that if you are not satisfied with the level at which you deliver basic services, it might not be wise to try something more complex. However, the time might never be right but the opportunity may present itself now through a change in personnel, a new economic development effort in the community, or a crisis that requires information.

## HOW DO BUSINESS PEOPLE USE YOUR LIBRARY NOW?

This is a good question for your staff to brainstorm. The answers will most likely astound them. Matters such as stock quotations, insurance company ratings, addresses of manufacturers, biographical information for speech introductions, hotel information for business trips, fax machine ratings, and laws on sexual harassment will be on their list. The difference between what you may do now and what you might do in the future is the way in which you market and deliver it. You're probably halfway there! In all likelihood, you have most of the required resources because some people, who are widely representative of the business community, are already testing the waters for you.

## WHO IS USING YOUR BUSINESS INFORMATION NOW?

That answer is the same as for any aspect of your services that you do not specifically advertise. People who use libraries without reminders are usually those who learned about them early in life and who are transferring that experience to their adult needs. You probably recognize the self-starter, the entrepreneur, the sales-person in between calls, the researcher. All that these people have in common, perhaps, is that they have previously learned about the bounty of library resources. And the difference between these users and those you still need to reach in order to be successful is that the current users operate self-sufficiently with minimal assistance from a librarian. They may ask for guidance or suggestions, but then they can go off to find the answers. They already believe that libraries can help them. The *new* business user will require an introduction to the services, a delivery of the information, and follow-up contact to encourage future questions.

The current user can become a "new user." For example, one management consultant prided herself on the research skills that she had already acquired. But now, as president of her own company, she could no longer delight in the hunt for information, as time equaled clients not getting answers. Also, the information world had exploded between when she learned her research skills and when she started her own business. She had to be introduced to a more mediated approach to getting her questions answered, and had to trust others to do the job so she could serve her clients.

## GETTING STARTED

In your initial planning for serving the business community or enhancing existing services, the following issues need to be addressed:

1. The right staff member(s) is the key to your success. Look carefully within your organization for the key players. Float the concept and see who responds. After you have grasped the essentials, explain to the staff how their job could change, how their work pattern would change, and the challenges they'd encounter. If the enthusiasm is still present, then forge ahead.

2. Make sure you have some flexibility in work patterns. Do you pay overtime so your staff can meet business people at early morning breakfasts or after-hours cocktail parties? The person who works with the business community may be required to complete researching a question just when the reference desk needs to be covered for lunch. Do you have the leeway to exempt a staff member from regular rotations on the reference desk if necessary? Business reference interviews take longer than the average reference question interview. Is your organization able to accommodate that? Do you as a supervisor have time to oversee it?

3. Your budget may need to be adjusted and reallocated. You will need to have the right reference resources to answer the questions correctly. On-line database searching is the best way to answer the majority of the questions. Do you have the equipment available for the reference library? Do you have someone trained in on-line searching? Are you committed to sending the designated staff to training and

to allowing for ample "practice" time afterward? Are you able to foot the bill for the breakfasts, luncheons, and dinners that staff will need to be at in order to network effectively? Are you prepared to pay for travel expenses?

4. You will need approval from others to enter this new arena. You will need to prepare carefully to introduce the concept to the library board, the municipal officials, and the business community itself through organizations like the Chamber of Commerce. Do you have the rapport and relationships in place to do that?

5. The services to support a new venture will have to be in place. Your telephone answering techniques and your ability to take messages, either directly or through voice mail, must sound professional. Do you have a readily available fax machine? Is there an e-mail account the librarian can use? Can you equip the librarian with business cards and with stationery that says "I'm here to do business with you"?

The following chapters will address each of these issues in detail. It is critical to be able to look ahead before beginning to plan a business service.

## NOTES

1. David Osborne, "Keynote Speech: The Role of Information in the Economy of the Southeast," *Southeastern Librarian* (Summer 1990): 57–59.

2. "Playing by New Rules: Nine Economic Development Realities for the '90's." Washington, DC: Corporation for Enterprise Development, 1990.

3. Lynne S. Ruetenik, "A Lament: Do We Miss the Good Life!" *Hartford Courant*, 5 March 1995, sec. C:1.

# BECOMING AWARE OF THE BUSINESS COMMUNITY'S NEEDS

When did you last ask a potential library patron in person what his or her information needs were? In my experience, librarians are more likely to send out surveys than to ask patron groups what services they need directly. It takes self-confidence to venture into a group whose members you do not know, ask for an expression of needs, and, at the same time, begin a plan to meet those needs.

Business people have changed as large companies have downsized and as the entrepreneurial spirit has returned to different parts of the country. The person who now needs information is no longer only the impeccably dressed, Harvard-educated MBA but may also be a recent immigrant to the United States with a minimum of education but with a great idea and enthusiasm. It may be the new mother who wants to use her skills to work out of her home. It may be the person recently laid off from a large company, devoid of support services for the first time, who has begun to explore new ventures.

Reaching out and listening to the business community you want to serve need not be intimidating. Think of the process as akin to talking to friends or neighbors. The trick is finding the right time and place to talk so that you correctly tailor the needed services, efficiently deploy your own scarce resources, and maximize your library's efforts. This chapter will describe several avenues of interaction that libraries have found to be effective in communicating with the business sector.

## FOCUS GROUPS

Focus groups, in their classic style or in a modified manner, can produce information valuable to your plan and introduce you to potential customers at the same time. Critical to the success of the use of this approach is the consideration of several issues.

First, you must establish what information you are trying to obtain. So that discussions stay on target, your questions should be both limited in number and clear. Typical questions could include:

- What questions do the people in the group have to answer from people inside and outside their company?
- What resources do those in the group presently rely on to answer those questions?
- What expectations do they have for the services of the public library?

It is not easy to get people in a group to discuss a topic with which they have little familiarity but about which they think they know more than they do. This is especially true of matters concerning the public library. For example, people who learned the basics of the Dewey Decimal system as students believe they should know all there is to know about using a public library. The risk of appearing inadequate or out of date in front of one's colleagues, and maybe the competition as well, is not inviting. Your approach to potential focus group members should assure them that they will not be asked anything they do not already know, and you should even include examples of the questions that might be asked.

Next, learn to digest the information you receive. You should know at the outset what capabilities you have available to act upon the ideas you gather. Question the practicality of any resource suggested by group participants. For example, if you hear that there is a strong need for information on advertising rates but you cannot afford *Standard Rate and Data Services*, do you have an alternative plan? After keeping this publication in its collection for two years, one library determined that while it was good to have in theory, the actual use it received did not justify its price tag. Luckily, they were able to resell it to an advertising agency and recoup half the cost of the volumes. The *Dodge Reports*, which follow the work, progress, and bidding status of construction jobs on a weekly basis, will be mentioned frequently in focus groups involving representatives of the construction industry. However, to be useful, this resource needs to reside on one's desk or be consulted on-line daily; visiting or telephoning the library would not be practical for typical users.

Finally, see the focus group setting as a two-way information street. You can market a service while you are gathering information. With a captive audience, you can introduce your service or at least stimulate interest. But if you are at the very early stages of involvement with businesses, you may not know how your service or product will evolve, so you should not risk leaving the wrong impression of what you can deliver. You should, however, promote the services you already have such as books, videos, city directories, and manufacturers' guides so that the participants leave with some new information.

Focus groups should be used to gather subjective information and to give you an opportunity to get to know the business community in a direct manner; allow an hour and a half to focus on the topics you want to learn about. The experience of some libraries has shown that focus groups can produce valuable subjective information about the business community and its needs. For example, the Business Information Center, a branch of the Gwinnett-Forsyth Regional Library in Norcross, Georgia (county population of 526,000), held focus groups prior to writing a five-year plan (see Appendix C) to improve services. The participants identified twelve areas of information needs:

1. Local information: the groups found this the most difficult area. Even if such information was available, it wasn't centralized. They were most interested in local company information, demographics, business licensing, and tax information.
2. Company information: local, state, national, and international.
3. Nonprofit organizations information.
4. Investment information and the ability to have it faxed to them.
5. Product information: suppliers and buyers of specific products.
6. International information: company information and import/export information.
7. Geographical and weather information.
8. Company credit histories.
9. Financial information.
10. Demographics: population and economic information at local, state, and federal levels.
11. Trends in state and federal procurement and acquisitions.
12. Topical articles such as banking legislation, managing technology, current events, and managing change.

Focus groups do not produce hard data. They are not scientific samplings. However, statements made in focus groups can be persuasive testimony in mounting a case for economic development support. Some statements that were noted in focus groups and subsequently used to support the plans included:

- "I'd always thought of public library services as similar to trash removal in our town—that it was available to residents, but business people had to secure an outside contractor."

- "Now that I know all the library has to offer, I plan on getting the value back for my tax dollar."
- "I'd always thought of the library as a place for story-telling, for studying, and for checking out books; I never thought it was for the business person. I can't wait to try it out."

One of the values of focus groups is that people can influence each other during their participation. You can observe how attitudes shift, and utilize that same technique when marketing your services. Focus groups seem to work best when the groups are homogeneous and the people do not know each other. Familiarity often inhibits disclosure.

With a series of sessions, you will be able to detect a trend and discount the aberrations. The Rolling Meadows (Illinois) Library, serving a population of 23,000, used such an approach as part of its business services planning, convening three groups—one for large companies, one for medium-sized companies, and one for the public sector. The discussions characterized the business climate, provided a sense of the community's business future, and identified the library's challenges in serving the business community.

Rolling Meadows asked the focus groups:

1. In 1999, you are being interviewed by the *Daily Herald* for an article about the last five years in Rolling Meadows. What will you tell the author? What changes have you seen? How will this affect the business community and the local government?

2. Think about a work/business situation you have had in the last six months when you had a new project, problem, or concern. What were your information needs? What information would have helped you?

3. How have you used the library to meet your information needs? (Follow up: What information needs would not be met if the library were not here?)

4. Think about information needs met elsewhere. Why did you use these sources and not the library? (Follow up: What kinds of information needs do you never seem to get met?)

5. What suggestions would you make to the library regarding getting information out to the business community?

The information needs of the participants were similar to those expressed in the Gwinnett-Forsyth Library's forums, but these groups produced interesting comments about obstacles to using the library:

- lack of knowledge of library resources
- lack of currency, especially with indexing of newspapers and articles; one month lag time was determined to be too slow
- the amount of time needed to go to the library
- problems with access: it's easier to subscribe to information directly; offering one library card per business is a major deterrent; the on-line catalog was not user friendly
- the need for interpretation of legal issues and regulations; copies of the laws and regulations alone did not meet the participants' requirements.

Some suggestions from participants in Rolling Meadows were:

- Use personal visits to business people to get out the word.
- Ask business people such as real estate agents and bankers to distribute library brochures.
- Change the current business brochure to list what people can find using resources such as *Thomas Register* rather than listing the source and assuming people know what is in it.
- Hold "business after hours" times at the library.
- Offer an area for "working lunches" so that business people may use their time more efficiently.
- Target marketing efforts to different businesses depending on the type of business and tailor the information to their specific needs.
- Let businesses check out reference materials overnight.

As an information-gathering technique, focus groups are valuable but carry some costs. Practically speaking, you have less control of an interview in a group setting versus with an individual. One member can take over and influence the entire group; the focus group works best with a carefully trained interviewer. The data are more difficult to analyze. And, most of all, focus groups are frequently difficult to assemble, as they are time consuming, labor intensive, and always involve some cost, whether direct or indirect. (For specifics on conducting focus groups at a reasonable cost see Appendix B.) You have to weigh these aspects against their advantages. Focus groups create a social setting for naturally sociable beings. The format allows for probing and clarification, and results are almost instantaneous. Still, if a library cannot conduct its own focus groups, the results of libraries in similar settings may provide a valid equivalent.

# MEETING THE NEEDS OF THE COMMUNITY'S CHIEF ADMINISTRATIVE OFFICER

The chief administrative officer (CAO) of your jurisdiction may be elected (such as a mayor or first selectman) or appointed (such as a town/city manager or executive secretary). Regardless of the way he or she got the position and whatever the professional status, these leaders need all the information available, and they need to know what information you have that they can use. Do you have an opportunity for regular meetings with other department head-level staff included in meetings with other department head-level staff from the town? If not, find out from colleagues how the CAO prefers to meet with staff, then make it your priority to become part of the team.

When you feel you have some information to offer, make an appointment and discuss how it benefits the CAO to keep you up-to-date with his/her concerns so that you can provide the best information possible. In case the chain of command is questioned, be sure to clear what you're doing with the library board so there is no misunderstanding about to whom you're reporting and the potential value of what you're doing for the library.

Once the CAO (the town manager) in Newington, Connecticut, became aware of what the library could do, he continually called upon the library staff for assistance. The most striking example of the library's worth came when the CAO received a call from representatives of an international company that was considering several locations in the area for its North American headquarters. They wanted to talk with him, they said, and would be in town in two hours' time. He immediately called the library for background material on the company. Reference staff located information through on-line databases and faxed it to the town manager so that he could speak knowledgeably with the visitors about their firm's operations. The company chose Newington, and the manager credits the library for that decision.

A town's CAO can also use the library's services and information for staff development in topics such as customer service or total quality management. The library might then offer workshops or other resources. Town managers should be educated to check with the library before purchasing books and other materials, since the local library may already have them in its collection. If books need to be purchased, the manager should be made aware of the discount libraries receive.

# SERVING THE COMMUNITY'S NEEDS THROUGH THE CHAMBER OF COMMERCE

A Chamber of Commerce is often the backbone of the local business community. But before you assume that is true for your locale, investigate carefully where power lies in the community. It could be in service organizations such as the Rotary, Civitan, or Lions, or in a special-interest group like the downtown merchants' association. And while an opportunity to be in a leadership role can be tempting, you should be aware of possible backlash if the taxpayer perceives (mistakenly) that "volunteer" work is being done during work hours.

Maintaining memberships in civic organizations for the library or its employees can be beneficial, but librarians should choose wisely which to join. Chambers of Commerce, for example, sometimes oppose their city government in matters of downtown revitalization, zoning enforcement, and spending. If you have a high profile role in the Chamber, you run the risk of going up against your city government employer.

A compromise to membership commitment is a liaison position to the Chamber of Commerce Board of Directors. In that capacity, you can appear on the monthly agenda and be considered a part of the board without jeopardizing your position as a community employee. This compromise can be accomplished if key chamber members are shown the value of the library's connection to their organization. Chairing a committee and playing a behind-the-scenes role may seem to give the library less exposure, but there could be opportunities to shine in areas where you as a librarian are already adept, such as in editing the chamber newsletter (and being privy to the information first), organizing a trade show, or cosponsoring programs at the library.

## THE LIBRARIAN AS CHAMBER OF COMMERCE PRESIDENT

For Cedar Falls, Iowa, it was business as usual to have an individual representing town government on the Chamber's Board of Directors as well as another person representing the university. Carol French Johnson, director of the Cedar Falls Public Library, carefully considered the pros and cons and, as a result, allowed herself to be elected president of her local Chamber of Commerce. Carol had been the library director in Cedar Falls for over seven years, had served on the Board of the Rotary Club, and had been on the Board of the Chamber of Commerce for three years before taking the Presidency.

Several factors led to her decision. The library had reached a peak in usage; in this university town, 80 percent of the 35,000 residents had library cards. Facing an upcoming building expansion, the library recognized that it had to be in close contact with every aspect of the community. The local utility had just installed a fiber optic network and the library was right there, creating Web links based on reference questions for the community. The library's staff and board were already accustomed to their director's heavy community involvement, so they were not fazed by the anticipation of more telephone calls and out-of-library demands on their director. Carol believes that the new age of information is a perfect time for a librarian to have the leading role in the business community.

Remember that the main reason to belong to any business organization is to network, to get people to think of the library, and to get people to trust you so that they call the library with questions. It also works the other way. If you know and understand another's business well enough, you'll be better able to deliver information that you know will be valuable. You truly promote the library's reputation when you say to a businessperson, "I thought of you today when I came across this piece of information—could I send it to you?"

## THE LIBRARY AS CHAMBER OF COMMERCE OFFICE

Ginny Bird, library director in Union County, Florida, took on the role of answering questions and turned it into a profit. The Union County Library literally runs the local Chamber of Commerce office. The population, previously at 6,000, grew to 10,000 with the addition of a 4,000-bed prison.

With the new prison came increased funding for the public library. After running a one-person library for several years, Ginny knew her goal was to get out into the community. As soon as part-time help was hired to free up her time, she started attending Chamber of Commerce meetings. The seventy members appreciated her proactive approach as she informed them of reference resources, distributed articles, and generally acted as reference librarian at their meetings. It made sense to all involved to pay the library a monthly stipend to answer requests for information about the area from potential residents and businesses, since the telephone, the fax machine, and, most important, the staff expertise were already in place. Ginny also relies on the

Florida State Department of Commerce and the business development office located in the local community college. Filling requests takes her an average of one hour per month. Ginny had the vision to take advantage of an opportunity to define the library's role and to propose the perfect partnership.

## THE LIBRARIAN AS CHAMBER OF COMMERCE EXECUTIVE DIRECTOR

Rural Savanna, Illinois (population 4,000), needed a knowledgeable part-time executive director to run the Chamber of Commerce. What better choice than the person who already answers many of the questions in the town? Part-time library director Karen Stott divided her duties between the two institutions and found the combination a natural one.

Her role at the Chamber office got her out of the library and into contact with business people who would not usually think of coming to the library or a librarian with their questions. She often brought these people to the library to find their answers and opened their eyes to the capabilities therein. But if she were not situated in that office and had not indoctrinated the Chamber of Commerce staff well, the library's resources would have been overlooked.

## STATE OF ILLINOIS LIBRARIAN/CHAMBER OF COMMERCE PAIRING PROJECT

The state library in Illinois recognized the value of partnering libraries and businesses and coordinated efforts to encourage such alliances. It developed the Library Partners program, which is flexible enough to be used in small towns and large cities. The underlying principle is that libraries alone cannot make a difference in serving the business community, and that it is necessary to link libraries with existing organizations having ties to business. Illinois chose the Chambers of Commerce of each community as partners. Both parties in the partnership sign a commitment pledge (Figure 2–1) after understanding the program overview (Figure 2–2). As of March 1995, thirty-five libraries had committed as partners and had plans of action outlined. For many of the libraries, it was the first foray into reaching out to the business community. For others, it was a formalization of what they had long been trying to achieve. (For a sample progress report, see Figure 2–3.)

**FIGURE 2-1    Library Partners Commitment to Partnership: Form**

## LIBRARY PARTNERS
## COMMITMENT TO PARTNERSHIP

LIBRARY PARTNERS is a program sponsored by Secretary of State and State Librarian George H. Ryan and the Illinois State Chamber of Commerce. The goal of the program is to strengthen the relationship between local libraries and their respective business communities, thereby promoting increased awareness, productivity and profitability in library, business and community development efforts.

### PLEDGE

We, the undersigned, express our commitment to form a partnership which assists our respective activities and improves our community. This commitment is based upon our belief that we can mutually add value to our services to patrons, members and clients by building a stronger relationship.

Our mutual activities will be featured in library and chamber meetings, publications and other forms of public outreach. We agree to report on our progress and strategies for the future to the State Library and State Chamber of Commerce at the conclusion of our first year.

| | |
|---|---|
| _____ | _____ |
| Library Director | Chamber Executive |
| _____ | _____ |
| Institution Name | Organization Name |
| _____ | _____ |
| Date | Date |

**FIGURE 2–2  Library Partners: Program Overview**

**Purpose**

To strengthen relationships between libraries and their respective business communities, thereby promoting increased awareness, productivity and profitability in library and business pursuits.

*Commitment to Partnership*

Upon your decision to participate, we ask that the library and chamber sign a "Commitment of Partnership." This agreement simply states a mutual commitment to foster a library/business relationship based on local needs. All activity will be directed and implemented on the local level. Any participation by the state will be by request and as a facilitator, including the distribution of a source book.

*Recognition*

The Secretary of State or his representative will visit each program site during the first year of community participation. A certificate will be presented to both the library and chamber in recognition of their efforts.

*Training and Outreach*

An Institute for Business Services may be offered for interested communities. This session will train libraries in new and exciting resources and ways to market those resources to the business community.

*Reports*

A written report will be prepared by each program site after the first year of their participation. The Illinois State Library will survey those involved, their planning process, activities, public relations materials and shared insights.

The Secretary of State will publish program materials and results to share with local, state, and national audiences.

*How to start*

Contact Catherine O'Connor, Program Coordinator, at the Illinois State Library, Library Partners Hotline at XXX-XXXX.

**FIGURE 2–3   Library Partners: Sample Progress Report**

---

## LINCOLN

### BRIEF DESCRIPTION OF PARTICIPATING LIBRARY

Library name, address and telephone number:

Lincoln Public Library District
725 Pekin Street
Lincoln, IL 62656
217-732-8878

Name and title of person coordinating program activities:

Richard Sumrall, Library Director

Population and communities served:

15,418; City of Lincoln, IL

What is your strongest service to the business community?

Business books, videos and audio tapes. We collect a wide variety of topics useful to the established business person. We also collect materials on starting a business and carry many state and national directories.

Descriptive features of the business patron populations (number of business contacts per month or year):

As a member of the Lincoln/Logan County Chamber of Commerce and Main Street Lincoln, I participate in meetings with these groups on a monthly basis. We also carry a regular feature in the chamber's monthly newsletter on the new business books available at the public library.

### BRIEF DESCRIPTION OF PARTICIPATING CHAMBER OF COMMERCE

Name, address and telephone number of chamber:

Lincoln/Logan County Chamber of Commerce
303 South Kickapoo Street
Lincoln, IL 62656
217-735-2385

Name and title of the person coordinating the program:

Beth Harding
Executive Director

Descriptive features of the business environment:

In a population base of 15,400 (Lincoln) with approximately 500 local businesses, the chamber represents more than 250 businesses. Our community city's west side, and a resurgence of activity in the downtown district.

Types of library materials/services used by chamber members:

Lincoln Public Library District provides the chamber reference materials in the chamber office, and regularly provides articles for the chamber newsletter, listing new business-related publications available at the library.

### PARTNERSHIP ACTIVITIES

Review of the steps taken to begin the Library Partnership:

• Contact program coordinator for additional information

• Discussion between chamber's executive director and library director

• Resolutions approving the partnership passed by chamber board and library board

• Establish a plan of cooperative activities

Past activities/events:

• Exchange program of reference and business books between the library and chamber's administrative office

• Survey of business community on library service (present and future services)

• Development of the library's reference and business collection available for loan

• The library and chamber will develop a brochure that details the different business services and sources available at the public library

• The chamber and the library will develop a long range plan for establishing online computer database services and CD-ROM sources at the library that will be useful to the business community.

# BECOMING AWARE OF A COMMUNITY'S NEEDS THROUGH THE TOWN PLANNING AND ZONING COMMISSION

In every community, some board or commission along with an assigned staff member has a finger on the pulse of what's happening regarding changes in land use. These changes may provide opportunities to serve the community or the prospective business owner. But how do you keep up with the developments?

1. Read the minutes of boards and commissions. As a public service, you could keep the minutes in your reference department for the public's convenience. Ask the person responsible for distributing the minutes to make an extra set for the library. You not only will be providing a service to the public but also will relieve some of the offices that produce the minutes from dealing with the public. When you receive the minutes, scan them for mention of issues that could provide opportunities for your services.

2. Stay in close contact with the staff member who is the assigned liaison. Have lunch occasionally. Read his or her reports carefully and comment on them. That person often has contact with people that need more information before they're able to file a plan. But unless that staff person fully understands what information you have at your fingertips or how you can take a question and turn it into an answer, you will stay an untapped resource.

3. Attend meetings of the commission when possible, or watch them on cable access television if they're televised. Listen for clues as to what information it may need now or in the near future.

4. Get to know the commissioners personally and let them know how you can help. Recommend books such as David Rusk's book on elastic and inelastic cities, *Cities without Suburbs*, or recent books on competing with superstores as you detect that someone might welcome the information.

5. Request some time at a meeting following new elections or appointments to make a brief presentation on how the library can be a resource. Then make sure you follow up with some information useful to the commission staff and members.

# SERVING THE COMMUNITY THROUGH THE ECONOMIC DEVELOPMENT DEPARTMENT

Economic development groups are sometimes volunteer boards, staff, or a combination. As with zoning boards, get to know those involved and how they communicate with the public. Create opportunities to help educate their staff about linkages and sources of information.

Dealing with an economic development body may seem abstract, because its job is to deal with the possibilities for the future rather than with the concrete current petitions for land-use change. Nevertheless, this arena is a place for you to shine. Once you understand its members' concerns, you can demonstrate that you have the potential to become an unending source of information. Remind them that the mailings they receive are meant specifically for economic development specialists, but you have the opportunity to peruse unfiltered information from newspapers, periodicals, and books as well as electronic resources.

In some communities, members of the economic development team go out and visit businesses. You could supply the background information or even offer to go along on such a visit (see chapter 7-Marketing-Direct Sales). This commission might need assistance in designing a packet to market the community or in publishing information about the community on the Internet. Now is your time to show off! Offer a demonstration of what other towns have done on their homepages and dazzle them with a World Wide Web demo. Take them to Palo Alto, Cambridge, Tucson, and Baltimore. Or try such smaller communities as Blacksburg, Virginia, or Hoboken, New Jersey. You will enlighten them and raise your status in one short demonstration.

The Parlin-Ingersoll Public Library in Canton, Illinois (population 17,000), found itself involved with the economic development board when the loss of a major manufacturer in 1983 cost the town 2,000 jobs. Although the library was independently funded through earlier generous philanthropic gifts, the library board decided to become more proactive with the local government and to contribute to the solution of the town's economic problem. Library Director Randy Wilson approached the director of community development, whose purview included economic development, and started working to provide and package the information to market the community to potential new businesses.

Randy and his staff researched comparative marketing figures using county profiles and calling other towns for utility rates. They then created a brochure and a multiuse folder that could hold a changing array of literature depending on the need or type of request for information. This successful process took about a year and resulted not only in a product but also in interaction among people who cared about the future of Canton as well as a new regard for the library as a source of valuable information.

## ECONOMIC DEVELOPMENT AND TOWN/SCHOOL/BUSINESS COLLABORATIVES

Communities today need cooperative efforts that involve as many entities as possible. The concept of a collaboration among the schools, municipal government, and the business community is a logical one for economic development. The schools must try to gear teaching and learning toward educating productive, flexible workers. To that end, the schools need feedback from employers as to what skills are and will be needed. Municipal government needs to cooperate with businesses to set goals, allocate resources, and plan space for the resident as well as the business person. If such a collaboration exists, the library can occupy a special place. The library already has, or should have, close ties to the schools and to municipal government. It would be advantageous to listen to the concerns of the group and offer library facilities for such activities as career nights, business forums for students, summer job fairs, and tutoring programs.

The Economic Development Department of Littleton, Colorado, took a decisive approach. Recognizing the importance of the librarian (or "economic intelligence specialist," as they term it), their New Economy Project hired a reference librarian from the public library to become part of the team, with the staff at the public library acting as a back-up when the librarian is out. The New Economy Project quickly realized the value of information to the success of their efforts. In other locations such services operate out of the library, but in Littleton's case the designated librarian remains available on a full-time basis to the economic development staff. The job involves soliciting questions, brainstorming with staff, and paying full attention to economic development issues.

In Fort Wayne, Indiana, public library business librarian John Dickmeyer plays a critical role in the annual meeting of the Indiana Northeast Development Corporation. Business people from all over the country who are considering relocating are invited to this regional gathering. The business librarian provides the convener with a packet of information on each company represented so that the sales pitch is better directed. He consults Dun's Market Identifiers (Dialog file 516) and also checks foreign ownership information to see which corporate entity will make the relocation decision in the case of foreign-owned companies. The role of intelligence gatherer is an essential one to the success of marketing an area to a prospective client.

## IMPLEMENTING A TOWNWIDE BUSINESS DIRECTORY

For years, the recurring question at the reference desk in Newington, Connecticut, seemed to be, "Do you have a list of businesses in the community?" The answer was always "No, not a complete one." The staff ultimately realized that the library had the best potential to acquire, organize, and disseminate such valuable information. With encouragement from the town administration and the Chamber of Commerce, the staff proceeded to gather data from various sources. The information, modeled on a *Standard and Poor's* style, was entered into a database and a directory was printed and made available for in-house use and for sale. (See chapter 6 for more details.)

Once the initial directory is compiled, it should be updated annually. The directory updates may include significant information that you can then pass on to others who can utilize it. Did the number of employees in a certain industry increase or decline? Were the number of fax machines or e-mail addresses on the rise? Was there a change in the product or service that the business provided? How many "return to sender" replies did you get, and was there a trend to be seen as to where the companies relocated? All this information is critical to share with town planners and economic development personnel.

## THE ROLE OF THE REFERENCE DESK

A person called the Newington, Connecticut, reference desk and wanted to know how to tie Zulu knots. You might ask what this has to do with economic development. The caller was a local hair stylist who wanted to get the edge on the market and had read that Zulu knots were a coming trend in hair styles. A good answer by the library could result in a thriving business. That's what supplying information for economic development is all about.

Reference desk staff answer thousands of business-related questions annually. Laws on workers' compensation, the address of a senator or representative, an article on asbestos abatement; all are examples of the inquiries received in the course of a week. While librarians are taught to keep everything confidential and not draw conclusions, they are not prevented from discussing questions at reference department meetings or investigating local business trends. The more such matters are discussed, the more the staff will be alert to changes in the economy and their impact on the community. All that information can be passed on to the municipal officials without violating confidentiality.

## DISCERNING THE COMMUNITY'S NEEDS THROUGH SURVEYS AND QUESTIONNAIRES

Caution should be exercised when compiling surveys and questionnaires so that the questions themselves elicit information you don't already know. You should strongly consider conducting them in person or on the telephone. Librarians report that people will rarely take the time to fill in a questionnaire that is left in the business reference section. Consider using questionnaires as vehicles to a discussion rather than as ends in themselves. For examples of business surveys, see Figures 2–4 and 2–5.

## FIGURE 2-4 Business Community Surveys

Libraries involved in the partnership program have used surveys to examine the information needs of the local business community. Two examples of written survey forms follow; these surveys can be adapted to address the needs of other public libraries.

### LINCOLN/LOGAN COUNTY BUSINESS COMMUNITY
### SURVEY FOR LIBRARY SERVICES

This survey is designed to help the library and chamber meet the needs of our business community. Please read each question and mark your answers according to your own business needs. This survey will help determine the development of the business collection at the Lincoln Public Library District. A brochure of business services and materials available at the Library will be printed in the near future.

1. Where is your business located?
   _____ Lincoln              _____ Atlanta
   _____ Mt. Pulaski          _____ Latham
   _____ Elkhart              _____ other (please specify) _____

2. How many people are employed by your business (full & part time)?
   _____ 1–4                  _____ 20–24
   _____ 5–9                  _____ 25–29
   _____ 10–14                _____ more than 30
   _____ 15–19

3. How would you classify your business? (check one)
   _____ retail               _____ non-profit
   _____ service              _____ education
   _____ manufacturing        _____ other (please specify)
   _____ government           _____

4. How often do you use the Library *for your business needs?*
   _____ never                _____ once a month
   _____ 1–2 times a year     _____ more than once a month
   _____ 3–6 times a year     _____ other (please specify)

5. What types of business materials do you *presently* use at the library? (check all that apply)

_____ none
_____ Illinois directories
_____ national directories
_____ business newspapers (*Wall St. Journal*, etc.)
_____ business magazines (*Forbes, Fortune, etc.*)
_____ books on starting/operating a business
_____ audio tapes on starting/operating a business
_____ Illinois law books
_____ other _____

6. What subjects do you want the library to collect for your business needs? (check all that apply)

_____ starting a business
_____ management
_____ supervision
_____ personnel administration
_____ employee motivation
_____ customer service
_____ accounting/bookkeeping
_____ legal issues/law
_____ other _____
_____ advertising/promotion
_____ market research
_____ site selection
_____ financing
_____ sources of supply
_____ computer applications
_____ taxes
_____ insurance

7. What format of library materials are you *comfortable* using? (check all that apply)

_____ books
_____ magazines
_____ newspapers
_____ public programs
_____ videos
_____ audio tapes
_____ computer
_____ other

8. What services and/or materials would you like to see offered at the library?

_____
_____
_____

9. Would you be interested in using a library pay-per-use online computer linked to different nationwide business databases?

_____ yes
_____ no

THANK YOU FOR TAKING THE TIME TO COMPLETE THIS SURVEY.

**FIGURE 2-5   Business/Library Information Resource Survey**

Which of the following types of information do you frequently need in your work? *Please check all that apply.*

___ basic data on other businesses (address/phone number/personnel)

___ background and opinion on current "hot" topics (environment, health care, etc.)

___ demographic data/marketing facts

___ information on changes in government regulations affecting business

___ other (please explain) _____

Which of the following information resources would be of help to you in your work? At least some of these things are available now at you local public library. *Please check all that apply.*

___ newspapers from major cities

___ newspapers from cities throughout Illinois

___ periodicals on marketing, finance, management, and related topics

___ corporate directories

___ census data files

___ company indexes on CD-ROM

___ bibliographies on topics of current interest

___ information on grants and assistance available to businesses and communities

___ other (please explain) _____

In what specific ways could your public library serve you better? (*Is there a particular resource you wish the library owned? Is there a certain type of service you would like provided?*)

# ASSESSING THE COMMUNITY'S NEEDS THROUGH BUSINESS AUDITS

The most direct way to become aware of the business community's needs is to ask! Librarians in Pekin, Illinois (population 32,500), did just that. In order to tailor their business collection to meet the business community's information needs, they created a "business audit." Led by the Public Services Coordinator and aided by a Library Services and Construction Act (LSCA) grant, the reference staff first evaluated the library's current resources. They found that fewer than 2 percent of the total library holdings, including the reference collection, were business related, and that, of those, 16 percent were considered obsolete. This discovery led to weeding and notations of gaps in the collection.

The next step was the most challenging. To do an effective business audit, the staff needed to talk to business people at their location. After carefully combing the telephone directory, the staff divided Pekin's businesses into ten categories: contractors, financial institutions, food services, media services, insurance services, manufacturers, retail stores, medical care, sales, and professional services. An insert in the Chamber of Commerce's newsletter inviting businesses to call and schedule librarians to visit them

## Getting Them to Know You

Convincing business people to give time to an unfamiliar organization or individual is difficult, as the Pekin staff found. When they saw that they would have to tailor their methods to elicit good results, they quickly put the following steps in place for the future:

1. Send a letter of introduction briefly explaining the project, asking the manager to participate, and noting that you will contact the manager in two weeks if you have not heard from her or him.
2. During the follow-up telephone call, let the owner/manager know why you're calling, how much time the project involved, what the commitment is on both your parts, and how the project will benefit the business and the community.

*Tip: If you are not talking to the correct person in the organization, ask who might be able to follow through with it. Cut down on calls by being direct and looking for closure. It may be faster to go on to the next business on your list than wait for an answer from someone not in authority.*

brought no response. However, after direct personal contacts by library staff, ten companies agreed to schedule visits.

Before the visit, librarians gathered information on the company. They then left the library to "audit" the resources the businesses use in-house, ascertain their knowledge of library resources, and discover unmet needs. Following interviews, a pattern quickly emerged showing:

1. Businesses had industry-specific information on hand.
2. There was a lack of awareness of library resources.
3. There was a need for services and materials that were currently unavailable at the library. Specifically, businesses wanted training and motivational video and audio cassettes; audio-visual equipment available on loan; and print materials in the areas of computer training, accounting procedures, and staff development.

The audit included a separate observation period during which, in theory, a librarian was to watch for unsuccessful information transactions among company personnel. That component proved awkward for all parties involved. Consequently, the staff thought that this observation component would best be used at the initial meeting or reconsidered as a necessary part of the audit.

After taking action based on the information gathered, library circulation of business materials rose 29 percent in a six-month period. Business-oriented additions to the collection were advertised in a booklet called "It Pays to Ask!" This publication was mailed directly to 900 businesses and distributed at a business breakfast and through the Chamber of Commerce.

There are a variety of ways to become aware of a business community's needs. Consider which of the above are applicable in your situation and utilize as many as you need to plan services to the business sector.

# ASSESSING RESOURCES

As important as it is to look outward to your potential clients, it is just as vital to look within your own institution to evaluate the resources you have or to identify the resources you need to begin. Personnel, equipment, collection materials, and even the building itself all serve as assets to a library's economic development strategy.

## STAFF TALENT

Staff talent is your most salient resource. If you do not have people willing to change their style of service delivery for this specific business/economic development population, you cannot proceed. If you do not have on board staff who understand and embrace the tenets of economic development and understand its relationship to their community and to their jobs, your initiative will not be successful.

Assuming that the staff share your vision, you need to assess their talents. You will need a combination of good marketers to promote your services and good researchers to provide your services. If individuals possess both qualities (which has to be the case in the smaller library), you have an added advantage. An outstanding business librarian once admitted that she considers herself a good business reference librarian but not a good marketer. She'd much prefer to handle the questions one-on-one with the client *after* the client is convinced to try the library for answers. This type of librarian needs staff support to carry out the role.

In preparing your staff, start with the basics. Have staff learn definitions and terms they will often hear. They should be able to deal comfortably with concepts such as venture capital, amortization, business plan, SIC codes, and demographic data (refer to Appendix A and the Glossary). Then introduce them to the tried-and-true resources (see "Reference Collection" section later in this chapter) and make up questions to test their knowledge.

The proper attitude is as valuable as a good knowledge of the resources. Librarians have a history of serving those deemed "deserving"—the unemployed, the young child, the person learning to read. When it comes to assisting corporate America, there may be an attitude hurdle at the reference desk, the feeling that service to businesses should not come from taxpayers' funds. Watch out for it and, better yet, anticipate it and address it head on. That service posture will need to be overcome by any staff member who expresses it, whether overtly or covertly. The important message to be conveyed to the staff is: *The better businesses perform, the healthier the community will be, and the better the library can serve.* Size of staff, depth of collection, and up-to-date facilities all pale in relation to a staff with a "can do" attitude. To help foster that attitude, make it relevant to your staff's personal situations. Most everyone is related to someone in business who has an information need. Ask the staff to come in with real questions from each of those business areas. Ask staff in other departments of the library to come up with questions. Once staff understand that they are impacting the lives of "real" people they know, the message becomes clearer.

One of the best examples that can be found of attitude conquering any obstacles may be found in rural Savanna, Illinois. With a population of 4,000, a total budget of $100,000, and a materials budget of $8,000, Karen Stott is known as the local expert for business information. Karen's philosophy is simple:

I look at the library as one of the many businesses in the community that needs to interact to survive. I don't need to come in with high-powered economic data to people in my small town. Just being out with the business people, knowing their needs and concerns allows me to connect them with the right resources. My collection is mostly practical "how-to" books and videos that I know the businesses want. I use interlibrary loan and referrals liberally and am fortunate to get year-old sets of *Thomas Register* and *Hoovers* donated. The most important aspect is feeling comfortable being out in the business community.

# COMMUNICATIONS

## THE TELEPHONE

Most of your questions from the business community will come via telephone. Is your telephone system up-to-date enough to accommodate all the necessary techniques in making and taking business calls? Does it have a voice-mail feature? Can you do conference calling? Are the people answering the calls trained sufficiently in both the features of the phone system and in the correct way to answer and direct calls? In some libraries, answering the telephone is considered a volunteer job. That approach will not work when dealing with a clientele whose first, and often only, impression of service is shaped by telephone contact.

Try calling other businesses that have customer service departments or give information, then call the library. How do they compare? Is the phone at the library answered as professionally? Are you left on hold too long? Where in the library is the phone answered? Do you hear babies crying as books are checked out at the circulation desk? Is the call bounced from one department to the next? Do you know the name of the person who is handling the request? Do you have confidence in who answers the phone? If you ask for a specific librarian who's not available, is voice mail offered? Or could anyone else help? Business questions tend to come early in the morning. Is staff ready to answer the phone at 9 A.M. or earlier?

A word about economizing: A feeling of guilt often lingers over the use of the telephone by reference staff for making long-distance calls. It is important to impress upon both the reference staff and the financial managers that information may be retrieved more cost effectively through a telephone call to the source than if time is spent searching through reference books. In the business world, a primary key to success is cost effectiveness; the same holds true for the library serving businesses.

## INFORMATION DELIVERY

Have you determined the best way to get information to the customer? Does your policy allow for faxing it? Can your postage budget handle more mail? If you mail something, does a professional cover letter and business card accompany it? Would you consider dropping off information to the patron at lunch time or at the end of the day?

# PRINT RESOURCES

The difference between print and nonprint resources is becoming more blurred daily. Have at your fingertips whatever format you can afford that gives you the best answer. Most business questions come in over the telephone. Where you searched is not important to the customer as long as you provide the best answer.

A small materials budget should not discourage you. Choose

your resources by consulting other librarians in similar communities and by carefully researching the needs of your customers. Find out which agencies provide information by telephone so that you can avoid purchasing what they have available.

While it is impossible to list a complete collection of business resources, some of the best sources are:

Lorna M. Daniells, *Business Information Sources*, 3d ed. (Berkeley: University of California Press, 1993.

Melvyn N. Freed and Virgil Diodato, *Business Information Desk Reference: Where to Find Answers to Business Questions* (New York: Macmillan, 1991).

Michael R. Lavin, *Business Information: How to Find It, How to Use It*. (Phoenix: Oryx Press, 1992).

Bernard S. Schlessinger and Rachel S. Karp, *The Basic Business Library: Core Resources*, 3d ed. (Phoenix: Oryx Press, 1995).

## THE REFERENCE COLLECTION

The tried-and-true print resources will continue to be the backbone of many libraries' business collections. Their reassuring presence advertises to the browser that you have current business information. In fact, one of the advantages of print resources over computerized databases and even CD-ROM products to the self-sufficient library patron is simply that they are so evident: it's hard to miss the multivolume green *Thomas Register*, but a single disk hidden in a computer's drive requires extra marketing.

Some excellent resources may already be in your library but just not shelved with those for business. *Fortune*, *Forbes*, and *Business Week* all have special editions with important business information. Either buy a second copy or set aside the following issues for reference:

- *Business Week*: the mid-April Special Bonus Issue
- *Forbes*: the last issue in April
- *Fortune*: the last issues in April, July, and August; the first issue in June

Business newspapers that are considered desirable are *Barron's*, the *Wall Street Journal*, and *Investor's Business Daily*. If they are not near the business reference collection, consider posting a sign to direct patrons to their location.

## Basic Business Resources in Print

Until computer searching comes within financial reach and its use is within the common practices of all public libraries, the following list of print materials is recommended for the basic business collection:

- Annual reports of area companies
- *Better Buys for Business* (consider putting a notation on *Consumer Reports* magazine alerting the business patron to the location of this business consumer resource)
- *Brands and Their Companies*
- *Business Forms on File*
- *Buyer's Laboratory Reports*
- *Directory of Corporate Affiliations*
- *Dun's Business Identification Service* (on microfiche)
- *Encyclopedia of Associations*
- *Gale Directory of Publications and Broadcast Media*
- *Hoover's Handbook of American Business*
- Local Chamber of Commerce publications
- Local city directories
- *Million Dollar Directory: Leading Public and Private Companies*
- *Moody's Investors Service*
- *Newsletters in Print*
- *Personnel Management Services: What to Do About Personnel Problems in [each state]*
- *Rand McNally Commercial Atlas & Marketing Guide*
- *Robert Morris Associates: Annual Statement Studies*
- *Small Business Sourcebook: The Entrepreneur's Resource*
- *Standard & Poor's Register of Corporations, Directors, and Executives*
- *Standard Directory of Advertisers*
- *Standard Industrial Classification Manual*
- State agency publications
- *Standard Rate and Data Services*
- Telephone directories for areas local businesses deal with
- *Thomas Register of American Manufacturers*
- *Trade Shows and Professional Exhibits Directory*
- *Ward's Business Directory of U.S. Private & Public Companies*

## CIRCULATING COLLECTION

Focus groups in Pekin, Illinois identified the same needs for circulating materials as did groups in Iowa City, Iowa—a community twice its size. The video format ranked the highest for training in management, computer software, motivation, and public speaking skills. Requests for audio tapes produced by leading management gurus were also high on the list. Demand for practical workbooks on setting up accounting systems, evaluating personnel, hiring and firing practices, and motivating employees far outweighed any requests for theoretical tomes and discussions of economic policy.

The message that we are now a visual and auditory society came across loud and clear. Libraries must rethink collection development strategies to accommodate that shift for the business customer who has neither the time nor the inclination to read. Selection of these materials is made challenging by the absence of reviews in the major library review sources. Instead, check the reviews of business periodicals and pay attention to the major speaking-circuit figures such as Stephen Covey (author of the *Seven Habits of Highly Effective People*). Make sure you offer titles in video and audio formats as well as in book format—or even *instead of*—if your budget is tight.

# ELECTRONIC RESOURCES

## CD-ROM

Resources in CD-ROM format are particularly suited to the library that has many business people accessing information independently. The search strategy is usually understandable and easy to use, and the product offers unlimited use once the library pays one up-front price. Information can be downloaded or labels printed. The installation of a computer network enables simultaneous use at many workstations, and some libraries allow dial-in access to CD-ROM applications from remote locations. Bear in mind, however, that CD-ROM information is more dated than that from on-line resources, whose companies update continuously (as opposed to the scheduled updates available for CD-ROM products). Carefully consider the kind of use your products get and the needs of the clientele before purchasing a CD-ROM or any other type of costly reference product.

Some basic CD-ROM products are:

- *ABI/INFORM:* an index to several hundred business and trade magazines. Many articles are available full-text.
- *American Business Directory:* a compilation of telephone Yellow Pages directories listing over 10 million businesses.
- *Business Newsbank Plus:* business articles and new releases from hundreds of newspapers, wire services, and trade journals in full-text.
- *Compact Disclosure:* selected text of documents filed with the SEC, price/earnings and ratio data, income statements, and full texts of the president's letter from 12,000 public companies.
- *Computer Select:* articles from computer magazines and industry journals.
- *Dun's Marketplace:* descriptions of 10 million businesses; allows one to create marketing lists, reports, and mailing labels.
- *Million Dollar Directory:* information on over 380,000 businesses; includes executive biographies.
- *National Trade Data Base:* over 100,000 documents concerning international trade from fifteen federal agencies.
- a residential and business telephone listing such as PhoneDisc, Select Phone, or NYNEX.

When choosing among print, CD-ROM, and on-line services, consider who will be doing the searching. If the primary searcher is the librarian, by all means invest the time and training in learning on-line services. If you have to accommodate many simultaneous users, consider a local area network (LAN) for CD-ROM products. Lean toward print resources if your population is still not comfortable with computers and will be doing the searching directly. Gwinnett-Forsyth Regional Library in Georgia found that one product not popular in CD-ROM as compared to print was *Morningstar Mutual Funds.* Despite its many features in the electronic format, the patrons preferred paper.

## ON-LINE SERVICES

Public libraries active in answering questions for the business community have estimated that they go on-line for approximately one-third of their questions. This percentage will vary depending on the librarian's familiarity with on-line resources and the alternative resources available, such as census information and government data on CD-ROM and up-to-date print resources. Having access to on-line searching through databases such as Dialog and BRS can fulfill the small libraries' greatest desires. But having an account and having the funding and expertise to utilize it are two different issues.

First, let's address funding. The budget for information services should allow full flexibility for the reference librarian. Transfers need to be easily made and allowed between accounts if on-line services and print materials are in separate accounts. Services such as on-line searching may not be defined as "library materials" in the criteria laid out by the library's fiscal authority and its auditors, but when an on-line database search provides the most expedient response to a question on a rare topic, you have saved a purchase, cataloging costs, processing costs, and valuable shelf space.

How much should be budgeted for on-line searching? Probably less than you think. Given other libraries' experiences, the suggested annual amount for libraries that have never used on-line searching and do not have staff who are comfortable with it would be about $1,500 at most. At this writing, there is an initial start-up fee of $295 (which includes $100 of on-line time, software, a password, and training) to subscribe to Dialog and an annual service fee of $75. After that, you can control how much you use it and how much you spend. Most libraries will already have a computer and a modem and the ability to share a telephone line for this purpose, so there should be little capital outlay.

It is important to have good, basic training in order to be adept at searching and to minimize the time (and money) spent on a search. Expertise cannot be developed or maintained without questions that require on-line searching. Here are some suggestions about developing skills and keeping them active:

1. Give librarians practice questions in various databases once a month to keep their skills active. For example, ask questions that could assist the library staff in writing reports and grants so that staff feel the exercise is "real."

2. Encourage the staff that receive questions to include others in the searching rather than keeping the question to themselves. A strategy session should keep the minds limber and prepared for a similar future question.

3. Circulate the new information on databases to all reference staff so that they are constantly reminded about the tool of on-line database searching.

4. Include on-line database searching on the agenda at reference department meetings so that examples of searched questions are shared.

5. Send staff to refresher training whenever it is offered. If it is not close by, invite trainers to use your location.

## On-line searches

What questions do public libraries throughout the country receive that could benefit from on-line searching? Here is just a sampling:

- Types of software opticians might use
- The address of the Partridge-Reddich Co. in the UK
- Music distributors in a tri-state area
- Names and addresses of errand service companies
- Venture capital companies in Connecticut
- The meaning of the slogan "No Fear"
- How to design a waiting room
- Stores for tall women in New England
- Retreat centers in New York
- Information on EDGAR and SEC filings
- Information on corporate gift buying
- The use of touch in psychotherapy
- Commercial realtors in Nebraska
- Mailing labels for Massachusetts colleges
- Florists in Newhall, California
- Information on Asperger's syndrome
- Food co-ops in Delaware
- The definition of a capability brochure
- Information on sodium phosphates in food
- Eating habits and food consumption in Germany
- Market information on the use of industrial water
- Information on the Negro League
- Addresses and phone numbers of snack and candy distributors in the United States
- Ford dealers with the largest sales volume in the CT, NY, NJ area
- Businesses in Connecticut with 500 or more employees
- Information on the sculpture *Awakening*
- Information on the Ben Franklin Partnership
- Information on lichen planopilaris
- Estimating software for construction business

All of the above answers were found using the Dialog system from Knight-Ridder Information. There are a number of on-line services that libraries use. They include:

- CARL—a computerized network of library systems and services including library catalogs, electronic delivery of periodical articles (UnCover—also sold as a separate product for interested libraries), summaries of broadcasts, and locally mounted databases; available through the Internet or to libraries that have CARL as a vendor
- DataTimes—a network of 1,000 news sources in real-time and past press releases
- Dialog—a large online service offering hundreds of databases as well as full-text access to hundreds of serials
- Dow Jones News Retrieval—full-text access to *Wall Street Journal*, *Barron's*, and other publications
- The Economic Bulletin Board—operated by the U.S. Department of Commerce; accesses files that contain trade leads, press releases, and statistical data
- LEXIS/NEXIS—full-text for newspaper, magazines, and other sources
- Newsnet—540 newsletters covering a variety of business specialties

Lorna Daniells's *Business Information Sources* provides a comprehensive list of business resources.

## THE INTERNET

The Internet opens up a whole new arena. At this writing, it is still not considered the source of first choice, but as more librarians get acquainted with its capabilities, it is sure to become an unparalleled tool. There are, however, some obstacles to its use. Access at the reference desk is not often available. Communications equipment, even that well beyond the local geographical area, can fail and obstruct use. But for browsing or putting out inquiries, there is nothing quite like a giant network of people willing, and often able, to assist you. The challenge comes in sorting out the reliable from the unreliable and then verifying the accuracy of the answer or the veracity of the respondent.

Here are some examples of how the Internet was used recently in Littleton, Colorado:

- to obtain a recipe for beef jerky made from turkey. The librarian posted a question to the rec.foods.preserving newsgroup and came up with a recipe for an entrepreneur who already had developed a market for his beef jerky product.
- to research the interactive-kiosk market using newsgroups to locate contacts in the industry.

- to find experiences and firsthand comments from customers of "switchless" resellers of long-distance communications service. This answer was unsuccessful at first with newsgroups, but the librarian joined a mailing list called "Market-l" and was rewarded with good response including a journalist from a national magazine who had an article in the forthcoming publication;
- to find out the potable water rate in Japan.
- to find sources with information on controlled business where real estate agents are originating loans rather than going through a loan company.
- to ascertain the names of people who would be interested in using Russian translation services.

As with other resources, you are as good as your knowledge of the sources you have. While more and more business people have access to the Internet at work and at home, the amount of time they have available to become familiar with its resources is very limited. You, on the other hand, have the advantage of being able to repeatedly navigate the Internet to learn which databases are reliable or not.

In order to take full advantage of the Internet, I suggest you first read *The Complete Internet Companion for Librarians* by Allen Benson and *Business Resources on the Internet: A Hands-on Workshop* by Gary R. Peete. Other resources are found within the Internet itself. Sheila Webber at the University of Strathclyde, Scotland, maintains a World Wide Web site of business sources on the Internet. The address, or URL (Uniform Resource Locator), is: http://www.dis.strath.ac.uk/business/index.html. Within that Web site you are pointed to company profiles, country information, discussion lists, and directories. In a quick glance you'll find sites such as the South African Stock Exchange, Hong Kong stock reports, Fortune 500 company information, electronically filed reports with the U.S. Securities and Exchange Commission, and a business background report from Dun and Bradstreet available on-line for $20 by credit card.

Networking among business librarians and economic development professionals occurs on two automated mailing lists, or listservs, on the Internet. Subscribe to the BUSLIB-L list by sending a message to LISTSERV@idbsu.idbsu.edu; in the message area type SUBSCRIBE (your first and last name). The Littleton, Colorado, economic development department maintains econdev. To subscribe, send an e-mail message to: majordomo@csn.org, leave the subject space blank, and type: subscribe econ-dev in the body of the message.

As you discover new sites on the Internet, develop your own "hotlist" when using a graphical browser such as Netscape. Then annotate it for the patron who might use your Internet station or for the reference librarian who works with you.

# THE LIBRARY FACILITY

Your facility itself may hold riches for the small- to medium-sized company. To the individual business person, your library is an off-site location away from the telephone and interruptions of home and office. Study carrels and other areas that are wired allow the use of laptop computers, calculators, and other items that require electricity and are vital for the mobile business person. Some business people enjoy being in a public setting so that they can look up and see activity but not be obliged to become involved in it. One business person even admitted that he preferred being at a table in the middle of a reference room to an individual study room because being in the public eye kept him on task!

Examine your meeting-room policy and make sure it does not exclude for-profit organizations. If it does, try to compromise and allow it for uses such as training a company's employees in how to use information sources. Just watch out that a company isn't going to make a sales pitch to outsiders that turns your community room into a sales room. Or, if your situation permits, be entrepreneurial and ask for a percentage of sales made from using the room. Figure 3–1 gives an example of one library's policy on the use of its meeting rooms.

## LARGE MEETING ROOMS

Even the person associated with a larger company may appreciate the use of library facilities for staff development sessions, which could occur in the large meeting rooms. Be alert if this kind of call comes, and be ready to offer to do some resource training to the company on whatever topic they're addressing. The fifteen-minute time slot before they break either for mid-morning or for lunch is a good time to pitch your services. One library was the site of a sales meeting for a local printer. Before the break, a librarian took fifteen minutes to describe the directories the library owned that could be sources of clients and to remind them of the array of visual resources the library had for ideas for their creative staff.

# FIGURE 3-1 Policy Statement for Lucy Robbins Welles Library Meeting Rooms

## I. Statement of Purpose

The Board of Directors of the Lucy Robbins Welles Library views the use of the meeting rooms as an extension of library services. The rooms should be available to the library community in its broadest sense and reflect the educational, cultural, social, and recreational role the library plays.

The Board subscribes to Article IV of the Library Bill of Rights which states that facilities should be made available to the public served by the given library on an equitable basis, regardless of the beliefs or affiliations of individuals or groups requesting their use.

## II. Availability of application for use

1. There are four (4) meetings rooms available for public use by groups.
   a. first floor community room (capacity—60 people)
   b. second floor:
      1. Richard B. Lienhard Room (capacity—16 people)
      2. E. Welles Eddy Room (capacity—20 people)

2. Meeting rooms are generally available for use during library hours. (See fee schedule under General rules and limitations, #12.)
   Availability of the meeting rooms shall be on a first-come first-served basis.
   The following priorities will prevail in case of conflict:

   a. a group affiliated with the library
   b. a Newington-based group
   c. a regional (greater Hartford or greater New Britain) group
   d. an out-of-region group

   The fact that a group is permitted to use the rooms does not in any way constitute an endorsement of the group's policies or beliefs by the Library or the Town.
   *Special requests for before or after hours use should be made at least two (2) weeks in advance.*

3. Organizations, other than library-related, shall not exceed four regular meetings during each year. The year shall begin in September and end in August.

4. Written application for each date must be filed at the Information Desk. It must be signed and returned to the library before the room is used.

5. The Special Services Librarian, in consultation with the Library Director, is authorized to determine the appropriate use of the room. In case of denial of use, appeal may be made to the Library Board.

## III. General rules and limitations

1. Groups using the meeting rooms will be responsible for:
   a. setting up chairs, tables, etc.

b.   proper supervision
c.   restoring the room to the same condition in which it was found, and
d.   costs arising from any damage or loss during use.

2.   Smoking is not allowed anywhere in the library facility.

3.   Refreshments may be served. In the first floor community room, the kitchen area may be utilized and must be left in the condition in which it was found.

4.   Alcoholic beverages are prohibited except as waived by the executive committee of the Library Board by applying one month in advance of the requesting group's meeting.

5.   If a group requires audio-visual equipment, the user must be thoroughly trained in advance and be held responsible for any damage to hardware or software.

6.   Storage of materials before or after the reserved time is prohibited.

7.   No material may be affixed to wall surfaces or tackboards without prior permission.

8.   Telephone messages will be taken for meeting room attendees **only** in emergency situations.

9.   The library reserves the right to seek references of any group before booking the room.

10.   Under no circumstances shall the sponsor of a meeting open to the public require sign-in of attendees nor should any follow-up contact be made at the sponsor's initiation.

11.   Groups and businesses may use the rooms for internal business meetings. Any group wishing to charge admission or make sales must obtain permission from the Library Director. Any approved group that charges admission or makes sales may be charged for the use of the rooms and/or a percentage of any revenues realized.

12.   Any use of the meeting rooms before or after hours, except by library affiliated groups, will be charged $25/hour or any portion thereof, payable within one month after the meeting date. A deposit in advance may be required.

13.   Anyone violating these rules may be asked to leave and/or denied future use of the facilities.

14.   The Library Board and the Town of Newington or their employees or agents are not liable for any claims rising out of use of this facility.

15.   No fees are charged for use of the rooms during library hours, however, donations to the library are encouraged.

IV.   **The Library Board reserves the right to modify sections II and III at any time in response to changing conditions.**

The room should be equipped with some standard amenities such as reasonably comfortable chairs and tables that can be reconfigured to meet the needs of the group, coffee and tea-making equipment, a source of refrigeration, and surfaces that can be used for posting information or tacking. A flip chart, write-on board and easel, and a floor podium and table podium are all useful. Other equipment you should consider include an overhead projector, slide projector, video-cassette player and television, video projection equipment, and computer projection equipment for a large audience, or a large screen monitor for a smaller audience.

If the participants are staying in for lunch, have a list of convenient caterers ready to offer—which will also help boost the local economy. If they are going out to lunch, create a restaurant map (see Figure 3–2) and a menu file for their perusal. Again, you are helping to fuel the local economy.

## SMALLER CONFERENCE ROOMS

Sometimes the smallest of meeting spaces suits the business person who wants to meet someone on neutral ground to discuss an issue. Home-based business people have found small meeting spaces to be good substitutes for a bona fide office. It means they can present a more professional image and do not have to clean the house! In some libraries, those same small rooms may be used by students studying in groups. This works out to be a perfect pairing, with most business meetings taking place during the day and students using them in the late afternoons and evenings. Be particularly attentive to the feeling and condition of the room. It should look "professional," without graffiti on walls and tables. Sufficient electrical outlets should be available for presentations and laptop computer use.

## EQUIPMENT

A valuable resource may be stowed away in the closet in your community meeting room. In Pekin, Illinois, an inventory of business needs turned up that businesses were interested in borrowing equipment that they do not often use such as overhead projectors, slide projectors, and a portable microphone. Bear in mind, however, that lending equipment for use outside your building could be risky, with an increased possibility of theft or damage to the equipment while being operated by a novice. In that case, refer back to the Library Facility Section above starting on page 44.

Some libraries offer fax services, laminating services, and computer equipment such as personal computers, laser and laser-qual-

**FIGURE 3–2   Newington Restaurant Guide**

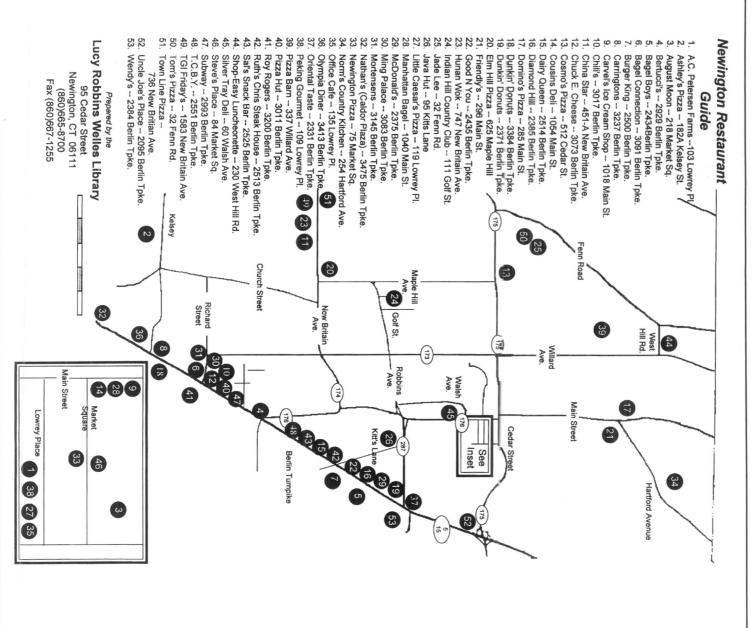

### Newington Restaurant Guide

1. A.C. Petersen Farms —103 Lowrey Pl.
2. Ashley's Pizza — 182A Kelsey St.
3. August Moon — 218 Market Sq.
4. Bertucci's — 2929 Berlin Tpke.
5. Bagel Boys — 2434Berlin Tpke.
6. Bagel Connection — 3091 Berlin Tpke.
7. Burger King — 2500 Berlin Tpke.
8. Carringtons — 3237 Berlin Tpke.
9. Carvel's Ice Cream Shop — 1018 Main St.
10. Chili's — 3017 Berlin Tpke.
11. China Star — 451-A New Britain Ave.
12. Chuck E. Cheese — 3073 Berlin Tpke.
13. Cosmo's Pizza — 512 Cedar St.
14. Cousins Deli — 1054 Main St.
15. Dairy Queen — 2514 Berlin Tpke.
16. Diamond Hill — 2385 Berlin Tpke.
17. Domino's Pizza — 285 Main St.
18. Dunkin' Donuts — 3384 Berlin Tpke.
19. Dunkin' Donuts — 2371 Berlin Tpke.
20. Elm Hill Pizza — 625 Maple Hill
21. Friendly's — 296 Main St.
22. Good N You — 2435 Berlin Tpke.
23. Hunan Wok — 747 New Britain Ave.
24. Indian Hill Country Club — 111 Golf St.
25. Jade Lee — 32 Fenn Rd.
26. Java Hut — 95 Kitts Lane
27. Little Caesar's Pizza — 119 Lowrey Pl.
28. Manhattan Bagel — 1040 Main St.
29. McDonald's — 2375 Berlin Tpke.
30. Ming Palace — 3083 Berlin Tpke.
31. Mortensens — 3145 Berlin Tpke.
32. Nathan's (Caldor Plaza) — 3475 Berlin Tpke.
33. Newington Pizza — 75 Market Sq.
34. Norm's Country Kitchen — 264 Hartford Ave.
35. Office Cafe — 135 Lowrey Pl.
36. Olympia Diner — 3413 Berlin Tpke.
37. Oriental Taste — 2331 Berlin Tpke.
38. Peking Gourmet — 109 Lowrey Pl.
39. Pizza Barn — 337 Willard Ave.
40. Pizza Hut — 3011 Berlin Tpke.
41. Roy Rogers — 3200 Berlin Tpke.
42. Ruth's Chris Steak House — 2513 Berlin Tpke.
43. Sal's Snack Bar — 2525 Berlin Tpke.
44. Shop-Easy Luncheonette — 230 West Hill Rd.
45. Silver Tray Deli — 60 Walsh Ave.
46. Steve's Place — 84 Market Sq.
47. Subway — 2993 Berlin Tpke.
48. T.C.B.Y. — 2551 Berlin Tpke.
49. TGI Friday's — 1583 New Britain Ave.
50. Tom's Pizza — 32 Fenn Rd.
51. Town Line Pizza —
      736 New Britain Ave.
52. Uncle Joe's Place — 2095 Berlin Tpke.
53. Wendy's — 2384 Berlin Tpke.

Prepared by the
**Lucy Robbins Welles Library**
95 Cedar Street
Newington, CT  06111
(860)665-8700
Fax (860)667-1255

ity printers, and scanners so that people can produce newsletters, prepare proposals, and respond to inquiries. The Liverpool, New York, Public Library (population 55,000) offers a scanning service at $1 a page which has proven very popular with the business community.

## STAFF NEEDS

Beyond the amenities provided for business people, do not forget what your facility needs to support the library staff. Each staff member who will be dealing with the business public should have his or her own telephone, voice mail, electronic mail, and access to a fax machine. Business cards and stationery will help the staff enter the business world. Indeed, as you read on, you will realize that one of the key ingredients to success is personalizing the service as much as possible so that business people feel they are receiving special attention.

In reality, the reference librarian may be away from her own desk two hours per day, but if telephone voice mail is available, it can keep that scheduling from being an obstacle to callers. Voice mail allows the librarian to access the voice-mail box, retrieve messages, and work on them while on duty at the reference desk, then get back to the caller with the answer in hand.

## OTHER AGENCIES

Providing information is enhanced by referrals and networking. This is particularly true with the business community. Look around your area. Who is nearby? Is there a business-and-industry association? Does it maintain a research department? Is there a business department at a nearby university? What about the staff at the Better Business Bureau? There may be private information brokers you should get to know. Do any of the local businesses have corporate libraries? Visit their facilities, extend an invitation to visit yours; you can set up a business information network with the research staff at each of those facilities.

# 4 TRAINING LIBRARY STAFF TO WORK WITH THE BUSINESS COMMUNITY

Those library staff members who interact with the business community are the most important aspect of service delivery. Far more important than having a fine reference collection or access to the Internet are your staff's abilities and having the right attitude.

## HIRING

Begin at the beginning, with the selection process. You may be filling a position that will work exclusively on business issues, or you may be restructuring the duties of existing staff to include business services among other responsibilities. At the interview, talk about economic development and its relationship to the library. Gauge interviewees' reactions; see what they understand. Ask about their knowledge of how the library receives its support, of where the tax base is, of the impact of businesses relocating both in and out of the area.

A corporate librarian for a major insurance company passes on the following tips: "Look for flexibility, creativity in digging for sources, a tenacious desire to find the answers, and a willingness to keep the customer as the key element in the transaction." A business librarian in a public library in Canada looks for social skills: people who can enter a room full of strangers, strike up a conversation, engage in small talk, and make the other people feel at ease. She believes it is critical for a person to feel comfortable with you to trust you enough to ask for important business information.

Ask prospective employees to read certain business publications prior to the interview, and then ask them questions based on those publications. Get an idea of their own background as it relates to business. Have they ever been in business? Has someone in their family? What kind of information did they need? Role play a business reference question.

# ECONOMIC DEVELOPMENT 101

**The Basics**

In training staff to work with business people make sure that they understand:

- the importance of information to the success of business
- that business is an underserved category of the population
- the language of business
- the resources
- a business owner's concerns such as cash flow, personnel, markets, and production
- how business service will fit in to the library's mission—combat the "but we do not have time" issue
- the difference between service delivery to other types of clients and the business person—the library is trying to help the business person to earn a living

Look to other agencies for help with training. According to Project Coordinator Nancy Welch, the Morrison Institute for Public Policy at the School of Public Affairs of Arizona State University played a key role over a three-year period in demystifying economic development to librarians. The Institute designed an introductory economic development course for librarians that was conducted by the staff of the state's department of commerce. Subjects ranged from basic terminology to the concept of enhancement of life. A section on economic trends put big business in perspective, since the Institute staff had observed that, without understanding the whole picture, librarians tended to see big business as the "bad guy." The Institute worked hard to help librarians understand economic development and strategic planning so that the library staff would become part of the planning process. The Institute also convinced other economic development figures of the importance of information to economic development, enabling libraries to move to the center of the activity.

In addition, the Institute trained librarians in communications—specifically in making public presentations, in handling the media, and in learning to speak in terms that lay people will understand—and in how to use business collections to answer the most often asked questions and formulate a business plan mock-up.

Encourage library organizations to hold workshops and seminars such as Arizona did. In Connecticut, the state library in co-operation with the Connecticut Library Association's Economic Vitality Taskforce held a series of four workshops. The topics covered were:

1. understanding the libraries' role in economic development, run by a local business person who uses the public library frequently and a librarian who is actively involved in serving the business community.

2. basic business sources, taught by a business reference librarian from a state university.

3. an Introduction to the Business Plan, taught by an instructor for small business entrepreneurs at a local community college and the librarian who teaches classes on resources available to produce a business plan.

4. demographic and marketing information, introduced to familiarize reference librarians with resources needed most frequently.

## BUILDING STAFF CONFIDENCE AND EXPERTISE

Not every staff member will appear well versed in the ways of the business world. You will not always be able to hire new staff possessing the requisite abilities. However, much can be done to build the confidence of current personnel for their encounters with the business population. Here are a few suggestions:

- Circulate business magazines and journals just as you do professional library materials. Order an extra copy of the *Wall Street Journal* for staff to read. Some helpful periodicals are probably right on your shelves—*Nation's Business, Inc., Home and Office,* and local business journals. Encourage regular reading of the business section of local newspapers. Discuss at staff meetings any business events that have a local impact. Assign different staff members to bring in local business topics of interest.
- Bring in speakers or local business people to talk about how important the library is to them and what assistance they value especially.
- Have staff attend business seminars on such topics as writ-

ing a business plan or how to market. Announcements of these seminars usually appear in the business pages of the local newspaper and through the Chamber of Commerce and regional and statewide economic development agencies. Get on the appropriate mailing lists so that you can post workshop listings for patrons, but first check them out yourself for applicability. Give each staff member an opportunity to discover what it is like to be the one in need of information.

- Have staff attend conferences and trade shows that cover topics other than library-oriented themes. Encourage them to ask those participants about their information needs and to promote the library's services.

## THE REFERENCE INTERVIEW

When reference librarians deal with business people, the reference interview takes on a different emphasis. Always the most critical part of the reference transaction, the interview is an important first step in gaining the trust of the client, which is necessary to get to the heart of the question. Some of that trust will come from the librarian acting in a businesslike manner. An exchange of business cards, attire that says "I'm an equal partner," and explicit acceptance of complete responsibility for the answer to the questions portray a professionalism that a business person has come to expect. A corporate librarian asserts, "There is a need to try to understand not just their questions, but their business and to make it seem that you share in their beliefs. The customer needs to view you as a partner. It could take fifteen to twenty minutes of asking about the question before you're really ready to find the answer."

As you can see, the time frame for a business-related interview goes well beyond the average three-to-five-minute period allotted per patron in most public libraries. While it may seem a luxury, the extended time commitment is in fact a necessity if the librarian is to guarantee accurate responses. Therefore, the environment in which the service is delivered is critical to putting both the patron and the librarian at ease. So set up a quiet office for telephone questions and a spot away from the hustle and bustle of the library for in-person queries.

Successful business librarians have found that they have to probe, encourage dialogue, and give food for thought. It is not uncommon to play a more aggressive role than in the normal reference interview by making suggestions for related areas the inquirer may not have considered. For example, if business patrons begin to talk about marketing a product, ask them the vehicles they use. They might not have considered trade shows or know that you have a directory of shows and dates unless you offer it. Some corporate libraries, as shown by the example in Figure 4–1 from Aetna Life & Casualty, follow up with a customer satisfaction card to their customers to assure satisfaction and to give them a way to get back to the librarians if there is a problem. It also serves as a reminder that the librarian is a resource for the next question.

Confidentiality comes into play in a critical way. Librarians should always respect the privacy of the patron and never repeat a question to an outsider or make suppositions about its motivation. The business person may be sharing information that will

---

### FIGURE 4–1 Corporate Information Center Network Evaluation

We care about providing quality information services and products. Your opinion is important to us. Please return this card to us with your comments.

A rating of 5 = *Strongly Agree*; A rating of 1 = *Strongly Disagree*

| | | | | | |
|---|---|---|---|---|---|
| 1. Staff understand my question and/or subject area. | 5 | 4 | 3 | 2 | 1 |
| 2. Response was quick and efficient. | 5 | 4 | 3 | 2 | 1 |
| 3. The information I received was focused and on target. | 5 | 4 | 3 | 2 | 1 |
| 4. The quality of the copies I received was excellent. | 5 | 4 | 3 | 2 | 1 |

5. Overall, the quality was:     excellent     good     average     poor

I used: CIC at Aetna Conference Center _____     CIC at CityPlace _____
CIC at Middletown _____     Archives _____     Education Warehouse _____

How can we improve?

Name (optional)
SBU/Department (optional)
Address/Phone (optional)

(Courtesy of Corporate Information Center, Aetna Life & Casualty, Hartford, CT.)

result in a competitive edge, a patent, or a change in financial status. You must emphasize at the outset that you will not reveal a confidence or any information you have found in the course of a search to anyone else. John Dickmeyer, business specialist at the Allen County Public Library in Fort Wayne, Indiana, likens this situation to an intellectual property issue. He makes it clear with his clients that he does not make any money from any of the transactions he will have with the library patron. He also assures them that no one will find out anything about the information search he is about to perform unless he receives a subpoena. He therefore keeps an absolute minimum of records. He will keep telephone directory–type information on someone and Dialog postings not attached to the name, except where charges have to be passed on to the patron, but even then without a specific data-base reference. Dickmeyer has encountered some challenges to his policy that could have caught him off-guard if his position had not been so clear. One municipal employee from the finance department challenged him about a long-distance call, but Dickmeyer simply said it was necessary to get information for a patron.

## LIBRARIAN'S EXPERTISE VERSUS CLERICAL SUPPORT

One problem a librarian working with the business community may encounter is a patron's confusion of the role of the librarian with that of a clerical person. It is not uncommon to receive a request to copy fifty pages and fax them within the next fifteen minutes. When you are trying to offer the best in service, how do you avoid this dilemma?

One librarian suggests that you set the tone right away with a statement such as, "I'm the business librarian, may I help you find an answer?" Another lets patrons know that searching is relatively quick because of his professional skills and that copy services beyond a reasonable time frame are not part of the pack-age. A request to fax an excessive amount will be countered with an offer to mail the material. Ensure that the business person un-derstands what skills you are utilizing. If, during the course of the transaction, you find that you need clerical support to carry out the request, say so; generally, it's the research skill that is miss-ing from the business, not the clerical support.

## ARE THEY ASKING FOR "TOO MUCH"?

Some librarians assert that they are expected to do work for the business person that the business person is paid to do. Indeed, some business people may take information pulled together by a librarian and pass it on (with a bill) to the client as their own work. The philosophy of one business librarian is that his job is not to judge what someone else does with information. He says that librarians have to remain ethical even when people whom they assist might not be honest. On the other hand, if he suspects repeated abuse, he will talk about time constraints to the patron. "Just because it's doable, doesn't mean we should do it," he states.

## QUESTIONS THROUGH A SECOND PARTY

Another common problem is the business person who asks someone else to get the information; the secretary calling for the boss is a common scenario. Some libraries have policies that require the person whose question it is to be the "asker," particularly before an on-line search is begun. Usually the reference interview will reveal that the question is not that of the person who is asking. At that point, the librarian should arrange a time to talk to the real information seeker. As one librarian succinctly puts it, "You wouldn't send anyone else to your medical physical, why would you send someone else to get the answers to important questions?"

## ENCOURAGING QUESTIONS

Delivery of service goes beyond the productive reference interview. It begins with getting the person to ask you the question in the first place. One librarian has found herself to be more aggressive than usual about approaching people who are looking at business reference sources or even just browsing in the general area. She has found that over 75 percent will accept her help once offered, but few would come to the reference desk when they failed to find the information on their own.

Other librarians use proactive approaches. Whenever one librarian hears of a new business in her town, she calls up and introduces herself and offers assistance. Another follows up on any new acquaintances he makes at business functions instead of waiting for the business person to call him first. Another delivers library cards in person to the company that has applied for them.

## NETWORKING

Networking outside the library is one of the best ways to make questions come your way; a word-of-mouth recommendation is one of the best kind. You can encourage those people you have helped to pass the word on to anyone they know who needs similar assistance. There are many opinions about the best way to network. Some common suggestions from management seminars are:

## Top Ten Ways to Network

- Make sure you are at the right place! Know the meeting agenda and who will be there.
- Participate in discussions. If you do not have enough knowledge to discuss an issue, ask questions for clarification.
- Do not waste time waiting to be introduced to someone you especially want to meet. Introduce yourself or find someone who will do it for you.
- Make new contacts. Tempting as it is to talk to people you already know, make yourself sit with people you have never met. Wait for most people to be seated rather than choose a table so that you make sure those who know you do not surround you.
- Invest time in getting to know people. They need to feel they know you before they will ask you informational questions.
- Invite your new contact to call you the next day to follow up on an offer you make.
- Listen more than talk. You will learn new ways to let people know what you have that can apply to their situation.
- Jot down notes as quickly as you can to help you remember people and situations.
- Wear your name badge on your right lapel. Your name is more easily seen when you shake hands. Ask permission to give your business card to someone.
- Follow through with a short note if you feel the new acquaintance could benefit from your services or if you would like to get to know him or her further.

Pat Tripp, business specialist at the London (Ontario) Public Library and instructor at the University of Western Ontario in business reference, passes on the following advice: "If you hear about a business seminar, call the organizer, offer to do a booklist, and talk to the group about related library resources." She encourages her classes to hone their social skills and to use small talk at gatherings to make people feel comfortable. Speak to them as people first, then let them know how you can help them as a librarian. People perceive librarians as very knowledgeable and can feel intimidated by them in a social setting.

## THE TELEPHONE

Someone you meet outside the library setting is more likely to call you for your next encounter than to see you in person. The telephone is one of the most used—and misused—communications instruments. A number of experts suggest the following:

- "I do not know" starts the response negatively. A librarian's job is not to know but to look it up. Instead say,

"Let me look that up and get back to you." If you need to know more about the question, go into the standard reference interview.

- "We can't do that" is guaranteed to start things off negatively. "Let me see what I can do" works much better.
- "You will have to . . ." is an annoying phrase to people. The only things people have to do are pay taxes and die. Instead say, "Here's what you can do" or "Here's how we can help with that."
- "Hang on a second" is a big white lie. Try "It may take a few minutes to get that information. May I call you back?"
- "No" at the beginning of the sentence is a turn-off. Instead, turn it into a positive response, such as, "I won't be able to do that today, but I can have it for you by noon tomorrow."

## ANSWERING THE QUESTIONS

You have won their trust and have solicited an interesting question. Now what do you do? Jump in! You cannot be timid or fearful about giving a perfect answer. Show confidence in your ability to the patron while at the same time checking with all your favorite resources—including a more experienced business librarian. Double checking those first few answers or approaches to questions will give you confidence. A midwestern librarian captured the trust of one of his patrons to such an extent that even when the patron went to work for Knight-Ridder, the source of many of the librarian's answers, he still insisted upon calling the librarian instead of turning to his own company!

## PACKAGING THE ANSWER

The delivery of the answer to a business person is far different from that used with a regular reference query. The more value you can give the data you have found, the more valuable you have made your service, says a Fortune 500 corporate librarian. Business people will not sift through extraneous data; mounds of information do not impress them. They simply want the answer to the question. One librarian recommends putting the results of the effort, but not the method of searching, in a memo and attaching copies of the source material.

A financial services librarian regularly takes information from a computer screen; sorts, clips, and pastes it into a word processing program; then sends it via electronic mail to the patron. He believes that librarians are in competition with desktop information delivery systems and must show the added value—information packaging—that is given to the answer.

As the librarian you must show the patron the added value of receiving information from you rather than an impersonal electronic database. A librarian with a vested interest in assisting the business person to succeed far outweighs in value an on-line service that simply sits on a desktop with its cursor blinking. That distinction is the edge you need to convince the patron that librarians are indeed an added value to the vast world of information.

## Referrals

It may be tempting to give the telephone numbers of other agencies that can help the business person in need. Treat such temptations as you would an introduction in person. Call the agency and ascertain that they indeed can provide the information. Get the person's name that your business patron should call, then call the patron with the information. This method ensures that you are giving the best referral possible.

## OTHER LIBRARY SERVICES

The business librarian cannot operate unaware of the offerings of the rest of the library. The introduction to library business services may originate in the preschool storytimes, or the shut-in service for a relative, or the genealogy department. A business person whose initial contacts with the library have been the result of personal, rather than professional, experience will have greater confidence in dealing with someone well versed in the many facets of the library. Small talk about other library services may lead into a reference transaction and set the tone for future involvements.

## BUSINESS PAIRING

In Newington, Connecticut, librarians found a powerful way to get over the confidence hurdle. They located three business people who were willing to be paired with a librarian for two months; the patrons could ask their librarian any business question that arose. In exchange for this "personal" service, the patrons were asked to fill out a form evaluating the quality and quickness of response and, more importantly, to assign a subjective dollar value of the answer to their company (see the sample "contract" in Figure 4–2). The results were astounding. The patrons asked an average of two questions per month—and thought that was a lot. The librarians, all geared up to serve, were underwhelmed! The

## FIGURE 4–2   Agreement for Business/Library Information Service

**Role and responsibilities of the Newington Library:**

1. The Newington Library will assign one contact person to the company for period of two months commencing Monday, March 2, 1992 and ending Monday, April, 27, 1992.

2. The librarian assigned will work with a designee(s) of the company.

3. The librarian will use resources available within the library and also refer the company to resources beyond the library.

4. The librarian will devote an appropriate amount of time per inquiry commensurate with standard library practices.

5. The librarian will train a company staff member in using materials deemed appropriate for ongoing use.

6. The librarian shall not obligate the company for costs of computer searches and other materials without the prior approval of the company.

**Role and responsibilities of the participating company**

1. The company agrees to seek information from the Newington Library for a two-month period.

2. The company will agree to designate individual(s) as the contact person(s).

3. The company will agree to perform an evaluation on each information transaction on the form supplied.

4. The company will make a good faith attempt to assign a dollar value of the worth of the information to the company for each transaction.

5. The company shall reimburse the library for any approved costs within thirty days.

**Role and responsibility of both parties:**

1. Both parties will agree to evaluate the progress after one month of participation.

2. Both parties will agree to final evaluation after the completion of two months.

3. Either party may terminate the project within the two month period for valid reasons.

_____   _____   _____   _____
Company Representative       Date         Library Director            Date

questions were no more challenging than any others they had ever received and required no resources beyond those on hand.

The three business people were completely satisfied with the responses, the staff felt they were ready to take on the entire business community, and the director knew the library could proceed with advertising business services without fear of failure. One of those businesses valued the worth of the answers at $1,800—for three questions in two months! That statement became a very powerful testimonial to the worth of the service to the business community, especially when the library presented its budget request.

## TRAINING PUBLIC SOURCES

Using an intermediary is one way to get practice in dealing with the business community. In Newington, Connecticut, librarians involved the counselors from the statewide Service Corps of Retired Executives and the Small Business Development Center. The library offered space for two regular meetings and asked in turn that the organizations allot twenty minutes on the agenda for the library to outline its resources. During the course of each session, counselors expressed surprise at the extent of available resources and at the knowledge level of the librarians. It was difficult, however, to convince them that the most valuable resource was the librarian and not to worry about remembering the title of a reference book. Librarians emphasized to the counselors that the best answers were found when the librarian completely understood the information need and was not asked simply to point to the location of certain resources.

At the end of one of the sessions, it was clear that the message of the value of libraries and librarians had been communicated when one business counselor announced, "I used to tell my clients to check with their banker, their lawyer, and their accountant before making important decisions. I'm now going to add their librarian to that list."

## TRAINING NONREFERENCE STAFF

Unfortunately, something done by one staff member can be quickly undone by another! In the case of serving the business community, certain exceptions to normal procedures may have to be made in order to serve the new clientele. New circumstances will present themselves; in order to handle them positively, the entire staff has to understand what the end goal is, not just as it relates to business clientele but to all customers.

Some situations that could occur include: circulation staff encounters a business person who does not live in the jurisdiction and needs to check out materials; a custodian feels cheated out of important cleaning time in order to accommodate that early morning breakfast meeting for a business seminar; the day-care center owner who was recently introduced to business services wants to take her classes to the library but is refused by the children's librarian because the schedule is filled; or the building monitor observes a business person tying up the public telephone making business calls, or is approached for an electrical outlet to power a computer.

It is important to empower staff to change procedures in order to meet unusual situations and accommodate customers. While such flexibility is important to serving any part of the population, it is especially so when embarking on a new service where it is impossible to predict all of the situations ahead of time.

Consider how to get staff involved directly. The circulation department could help register people for library cards at a business fair or in a new office building. Circulation and children's staff could help establish deposit collections at office parks, Chamber of Commerce offices, day-care centers, or travel agencies. The more members of the staff buy into a new service, the more likely it will be to succeed.

# GETTING YOUR FOOT IN THE DOOR

You have oriented your staff and expanded your collection to give better service to the business community. You feel well trained and ready to offer your services. But you do not yet have the opportunity to show what you really can do. Unlike, for example, setting up a service for shut-ins, to begin services to the business community you must establish yourself in a network that may exist among people who meet often for business reasons. Going into the economic development field with information services means convincing people who have functioned for years without you that you can enhance what they already offer.

---

**Getting Your Foot in the Door**

John Gruidl, at the Illinois Institute for Rural Affairs, works closely with Illinois librarians in rural areas and encourages their role in economic development. He offers the following advice:

1. Become a member of the Chamber of Commerce or local development organization. You can't plan services until you know the players and the needs.
2. Start with the role of providing information, because all businesses are dependent on it. He believes that the librarian is likely to be the most talented person in the rural community.
3. Develop a network of other librarians who are engaged in the same strategies so that you can support each others' efforts.
4. Make sure your efforts are not perceived as a threat, but as a way to support the community.
5. Get yourself appointed to a board or commission as a citizen and then use your librarian skills.
6. And finally, remember that it won't happen overnight. Relationships take time to grow and for the trust to develop.

---

While it may be easier to get a foot in the door in smaller communities, which have fewer people interested in serving the community and maybe less of a political quagmire to get through, the same principles apply whether the community is large or small.

# FIND AN ADVOCATE

How do you break into the inner circle? One way is to identify an advocate who will provide access to the people with whom you need to network. Think of your situation as being similar to becoming a country club member. Sponsorship by someone whose reputation is already established endorses your services and, more importantly, you. That advocate can get you invitations to the right meetings and gatherings, introduce you to others, and promote the library and its services.

How do you find such a guardian angel? You may be looking for one person or many, depending on the size of the community. Ask people you know about leaders in business organizations. Ask if they are receptive to new ideas. Pay close attention to their library use patterns or those of their families. Do not overlook the obvious—someone could be related to a staff member. Encourage your library board or Friends organization to suggest people who might assist, then have them introduce you. Ask library board members active in business to invite you to social events they host. Cocktail chatter during which people are relaxed gives you a better opening than the formal meeting.

## Pointers for Developing Advocates

- Invite potential advocates to lunch to discuss your plans for business services. Pull them into your thinking so they own a piece of the plan.
- Assemble leading business minds for a discussion at one of their locations after you have made an initial connection. Tell them who is expected; you will find that no one will want to be left out.
- Identify people who are eager to listen to what you have to say; the ones who are mainly interested in talking about themselves and their business operations probably aren't good candidates for becoming an advocate.
- After you have identified some advocates, help them champion your cause. Demonstrate the kinds of information you can retrieve with examples of real questions. Make these people partners, so they not only carry the enthusiasm but also "sell" what you can deliver.
- Learn to listen to these people. They are in a position to offer knowledgeable insights about the current issues, the needs of the business community and who is involved in what.
- When you hear something that perks you up, do not hesitate to ask for more information or for introductions to the people who are mentioned.

How do you persuade someone as valuable as an advocate to spend time with you? That's where your sales ability comes into play. Any new business relationship has to have benefits for both parties, and there are many ways in which you can repay your advocate for time and advice. Remember to explain to your advocate what you are asking him/her to help you sell and to speak in terms of benefits to the business person, not the features of information sources. For example, don't tell someone that by using Dialog you can access hundreds of databases. Instead point out that you can get a listing of all the laundromats in the tristate area to help expand the business for an appliance repair service. Remember that business people have been functioning without you for years. They can continue to rely on information sources they've always used—or they can give you a chance to show what you can do. The critical factor is trust.

# SELECTIVE DISSEMINATION OF INFORMATION

SDI, the selective dissemination of information, has always been a librarian's secret weapon. What is SDI? In this case, it is specifically choosing and sending information that you think will be of interest to the business person you have just met. It gives you an opportunity to remind people you're there and to call attention to the value of knowing you and being associated with your services.

Start SDI, but send material in usable form! Take a chapter out of corporate librarians' books: highlight, underline, and condense information for your customer to read quickly. An entire book on exporting to the Pacific Rim, as terrific as it may be, will sit on a busy person's desk long past the due date. *Send something that doesn't have to be returned;* include your business card with a note asking if you can provide more material or saying that you'll call later to see if the information was helpful. Remember the nature of SDI; the recipients didn't ask for it, so don't expect them to drop everything and pay full attention to whatever you send. But don't underestimate the aftereffect of peoples' surprise at what the library can supply and what you as a librarian understand about their business information needs.

## Egos

Caution! You're around to supply information, to be called upon as a knowledgeable source, not to make anyone feel inadequate. If the people to whom you're trying to get information sense that your effort is mostly an opportunity to show how much you know, they won't ask. The risk of feeling inadequate is far more threatening to people than is being without information.

Don't let your enthusiasm for the service overwhelm anyone. Instead:

- stop to see who truly welcomes your presence
- time your appearances; don't try to be everywhere
- ask questions
- learn to read body language
- inform people in private, then let them give the information
- praise companies for seeking information

Books on communication may help, if only for a refresher on what we already know. And considering the business environment, current titles such as *Men Are from Mars, Women are from Venus* by John Gray and *You Just Don't Understand* by Deborah Tannen could be very helpful.

Invite business people to speak at conferences for librarians. It will flatter them to be asked and give them a reason to think about how important information is. Ride in the car together to the conference location. How often do you get an opportunity to have an exclusive audience with a business person?

Getting past one's ego is a critical key to success in providing service to the business community. You have to be perceived as a partner with something valuable to offer, something that enhances another's operation.

## OTHER OPPORTUNITIES

There may be some other methods you haven't considered that will get you noticed in your business community. A term on a community board or commission will seat you alongside business people. Let the right people know that you will serve or even that you could represent your community at an out-of-town meeting or two. If your community regularly staffs trade show booths, offer to help out.

Getting into print in the right places can't hurt. In Connecticut, the editor of *Conntact*, a publication for businesses using SNET (the statewide telephone company), was convinced of the need for library business services. He encouraged SNET to sponsor a full-page ad on the subject (see Figure 5–1) in *Comntact*. The ad was created by a public relations firm that knew from personal experience how instrumental libraries were. A series of ads has continued in each issue of the publication, which is distributed to every business phone customer in the state.

Conferences dealing with business and economic development are publicized in the business section of the local newspaper. Attend a few. As part of the audience, you can hear people's concerns and needs. Casual conversations allow you quietly to pitch your services. Invite town officials to go along with you. Make sure you have business cards with you and that you follow up on

**FIGURE 5–1   Advertisement to Promote Library Business Services**

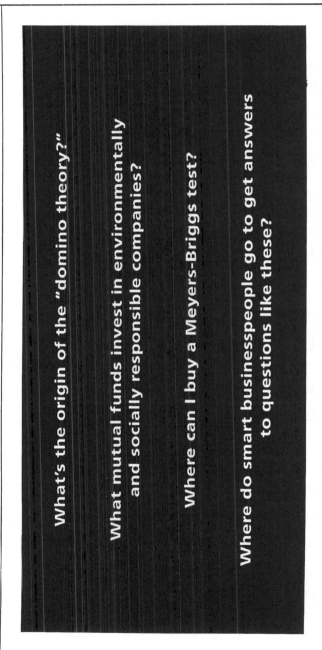

The library. Surprised? Think about it. The library is filled with information. That's right, even business information. And it's free. So the next time you need to know who coined the phrase "think and grow rich" or have any other business questions, call or visit your local library.

**Connecticut Library Association**
*Your business information resource.*

Ad Created By: The Idea Factory, Inc., Newington, CT

Note: The Idea Factory, Inc., is a marketing communications and organizational creativity consulting and training firm.

any contacts you make. As someone in the audience, you have the opportunity to ask cogent questions of a presenter and make comments. This can be an effective way to inform the rest of the audience of the library's resources and your own abilities.

People in other fields can help you both to understand your community's business needs and to open up networking opportunities. An appointment with a bank's economist can be an education in economic conditions. Don't be threatened. If your Economics 101 course seems like a long time ago, or if it never happened at all, never mind. Just explain that you're there to learn. Faculty members in the local business school may also be practicing business people. Talk to them about the concerns of their students, particularly those returning to school from the business world. In exchange, you can offer them the chance for an independent study of the effect of your services to businesses. Newspaper reporters can be a particularly rich source of information. They interact with different people daily and may have some suggestions based on their interviews with representatives of your target customer base. If you've done your homework, by now you should have assessed the territory, understood where you fit in, and what strengths and weaknesses exist in the economic front in your locale.

## MAKE YOURSELF INDISPENSABLE

That's what John Dickmeyer, business specialist at the library in Fort Wayne, Indiana, believes. He advocates looking for the "lean and mean" people who need assistance. Staffs of business-support organizations are only so big, so there are bound to be gaps in their expertise. If you find that a Chamber of Commerce is strong in paying attention to retailers but can't assist manufacturers equally well, specialize and market accordingly.

Find the weak link in the service delivery. It's impractical for a business-support organization to have a bona fide research person on their staff. Find out how you can assist and do a bang-up job. Dickmeyer recommends a twenty-four-hour turnaround time, with personal delivery to the client if necessary.

Another organization that most likely does not have a researcher on board is your local municipal government. Again, Fort Wayne, Indiana, shines in this area. When the library discovered the city's frustration with the discrepancy between city council districts and the census boundaries, the reference staff reformatted the census information so that it could be made into usable tracts for local officials. The city planning departments and economic development departments in Fort Wayne keep track of all their questions and how they're answered. Not surprisingly, answers to the hard informational questions came from the library rather than the departments themselves. But the Fort Wayne library doesn't just wait for the questions to come. It sends demographic information to the town planning and economic development departments throughout the year.

Other ideas for ways to assist municipalities were compiled for an annual municipal league conference in Connecticut. Some of the suggestions are relatively simple for libraries, but they give municipal officials a way both to point to library service as an integral part of government and to keep the vital service in mind throughout the year:

- Place all minutes of board and commission on file at the library.
- Use the library as the main distribution point for annual reports and other municipal give-away documents.
- Make the library a polling location.
- Place copies of the Charter and Code of Ordinances in the library.
- Have the library collect, bind, and microfilm town annual reports.
- Use the library's consumer information when evaluating products or writing specifications.
- Place examination promotion books on reserve at the library for police, firefighters, and others to use.
- Have the library collect management books and information for municipal staff.

Grant writing may provide yet another great opportunity to offer essential information. Most grants require statistics and evidence of need based on population. Let municipal departments and nonprofit organizations that write grant requests know of your resources, and you can find yourself an indispensable part of the process.

# WHAT SPECIFIC SERVICES CAN MY LIBRARY PROVIDE?

Once the foundation for enhanced business services is laid, it is time to roll up your sleeves and really get to work. This chapter describes some successful business-oriented projects undertaken by public libraries that have become involved in the local economic development process. The number and nature of specific services will vary from community to community and from library to library, but they have one thing in common: They work!

## TOWN BUSINESS DIRECTORY

The public library in Newington, Connecticut, began its involvement in economic development with the compilation of a town business directory. Having been asked repeatedly, "Does the town have a business directory?" the library decided to tackle the job. The library seemed the logical author because the local Chamber of Commerce was a volunteer organization without staff, and because no town economic development department existed at the time. While the research and production continues to be time consuming and labor intensive, the publication is an example of local information at its best and outshines the standard sources of business information. Was it an easy task to undertake? No! Was it worth it? Yes! What pay-offs have been received from the effort?

1. The library is now the prime information source for prospective businesses who want to check on the local competition and for local businesses who want to do business with each other.
2. The library holds the statistics on the number of employees in the town, the sales volume, the types of businesses and the number in any given field. The exact number of businesses was not known until this project was undertaken!
3. The library has a reason to communicate constantly with businesses through annual updating procedures. New busi-

nesses receive a telephone call asking for the initial information. These calls also provide an opening to introduce library services.

4. The mailing list generated allows the library to send out information to all businesses or any segment with ease.

5. Income is generated by selling the directory and mailing labels from the list. While the directory is available for use in the library as well as in circulation, the library holds the data and does not sell or loan the raw data in disk form.

If you have a similar void in your town and can choose only one activity, let it be this one!

## Creating a Business Directory

The Newington reference staff began with the personal property tax list from the assessor's office, then combed regional, state, and national business directories, telephone books, and local newspapers to create the initial list. A questionnaire was sent to 1,000 companies, 350 of which returned the questionnaire. Press releases alerted business people who did not receive the mailing to contact the library if they wished to be included in the directory. Next came the tedious follow-up: a combination of staff and volunteers called all the unresponding businesses to gather the information.

After the first year, the job became easier. Businesses understand why they're being asked to fill out the information. They no longer suspect that the canvass may be a marketing ploy to sell a product or that the town is checking up on them in some way. The directory's listings are used every other month by the library to mail a business newsletter, and returns from the post office help keep the database current.

Detective work and ingenuity are necessary to track down new businesses. Some helpful sources include real estate transactions, the police department, utility companies, and the Yellow Pages. Home-based businesses are the most elusive but can be found through entrepreneurial support groups. Suppliers of goods and services such as local printers can also provide valuable information. And advertise that you have a directory.

The public library in Southfield, Michigan, took a different tack. Its directory (Figures 6-1, 6-2) lists the locale's top 100 companies, the Fortune 500 companies, the major employers, foreign-owned companies, and banking institutions.

Each library has to examine the community's needs and its own resources before tackling such a project. While the costs involved might be relatively substantial, funding for such a project may

**FIGURE 6–1  Sample Page from Directory of Top One Hundred Companies in Southfield, Michigan**

The companies listed here were located by computer search of *Dun & Bradstreet* and *Standard & Poor's* databases from *Crains Detroit Business* and other sources. They have been chosen according to their financial net worth, or their sales or revenues figures. All information contained has been checked with the individual companies. *Please Note*: Not all companies wished to be listed here, while others requested their financial status be kept private. Those requests have been honored.

**Advance Watch Co. Ltd**
26400 W. Eight Mile Rd.
Southfield, MI 48034.
Phone: (810) 353-5130
Type: Manufacturers, wholesale imports and distributors of watches, clocks and pens.
# SFLD. Employees: 100  Total Emp: 800
Sales: N.A.
President: Marc Schechter
Headquarters: World Headquarters

**Ahresty of America Corporation**
27777 Franklin Rd., Suite 930
Southfield, MI 48034
Phone: (810) 350-3520
Type: Aluminum Die Castings - Sales
# SFLD. Employees: 5    Total Emp: 650 approximately
Sales: $31.2 million
General Manager (Local): Shinichi Endo
Headquarters: U.S. Headquarters, Sales Office

**Allied Signal Automotive**
20650 Civic Dr.
Southfield, MI 48086
Phone: (810) 827-5000
Type: Manufacturing, Independent automotive suppliers.
# SFLD. Emp: 130 Total Emp: 38,000
Sales: N.A.
President: Ralph E. Reins
Headquarters: World headquarters for automotive; administrative/sales

**Allstate Insurance Companies**
100 Galleria Officentre, Suite 300
Southfield, MI 48034
Phone: (810) 351-7000
Type: Full line of insurance, auto and homeowners, casualty
# SFLD. Empl: 335 Total Empl: 53,000
Sales: N.A.
Chairman of Board: Jerry Shoate

**FIGURE 6-2   Sample Page from Directory of Foreign-Owned Companies in Southfield, Michigan**

The companies listed here were identifiable readily as foreign-owned, using information from the Oakland County Economic Development Division and sources such as the Japanese Business Society of Detroit. This list may not be complete.

**Ahresty of America**
Parent Company: Ahresty Corporation
City of Origin: Tokyo.          Country: Japan
Local Address: 27777 Franklin Rd, Suite 930.     Zip: 48034
Phone: (810) 350-3520
Product/Service: Sales Office for Aluminum Die Casting

**Alcan Rolled Products Co.**
Parent Company: Alcan Aluminum Ltd.
City of Origin: Montreal.     Country: Canada
Local Address: 4000 Town Center, Suite 680     Zip: 48075
Phone: (810) 354-0790
Product/Service: Sales Office, Automotive Aluminum Products

**Alitalia Airlines**
Parent Company: Alitalia Airlines I.R.I
City of Origin: Rome.          Country: Italy
Local Address: 3000 Town Center.     Zip: 48075
Phone: (810) 353-6520
Product/Service: Airline Sales Office

**Amdahl Corporation**
Parent Company: Fujitsu Co. Ltd./Amdahl
Country: Japan
Local Address: 3000 Town Center, Suite 3100     Zip: 48075
Phone: (810) 358-4440
Product/Service: Sales Service for IBM Mainframe Storage Equipment

**Apollo America Corporation**
Parent Company: Idemitsu Kosan Co. Ltd.
City of Origin: Tokyo.          Country: Japan
Local Address: 2000 Town Center, Suite 1450     Zip: 48075
Phone: (810) 355-0666
Product/Service: Sales of Chemicals, Lubrication Manufacture

**Asahi Travel**
Parent Company: Asahi Travel
Country: Japan
Local Address: 23023 Beech Rd     Zip: 48034
Phone: (810) 357-2266
Product/Service: Sales for Travel

exist from sources other than the library's budget. The need for a directory is often so strong that another government department or agency may be willing to underwrite the cost in exchange for the library's expertise and close association with the community.

## BUSINESS NEWSLETTER

You may already produce a newsletter for general library users. If so, you have the tools in place to start a business newsletter. But keep in mind that the quality and content are critical: this publication will compete with business advertising for attention and will need to be mailed out to have the maximum impact.

What should you put in? Short, to-the-point paragraphs, relevant tips, examples of questions answered for other businesses, profiles of how businesses use library services, and pictures or illustrations are all effective newsletter components (see Figure 6–3). What should you downplay? Recommending books—such material only perpetuates the misconception that the library offers only printed, bound materials.

Stress how convenient it is to get information through the business reference service at the library. Make copies of the newsletter available throughout the library facility and in other areas where business people gather.

Tip: Newsletters are rarely read unless the value of the institution is already proven to the recipient. This is not the activity to tackle first. Wait until you've made a name for yourself.

## COMMUNITY INFORMATION PACKETS

Personnel departments want to keep those carefully chosen employees once they're hired. The library can help make new workday residents feel welcome with a packet of information on the town in which they spend many of their waking hours. You can also make the information available to new residents of your community and thus have a multiple-use packet. Call a sampling of personnel officers to find out what information should be included. Often a listing of restaurants, banks, day-care facilities, and services such as hair stylists, dry cleaners, and shoe repair locations

**FIGURE 6-3 Examples of Articles from *Friends in Business Newsletter*, Newington, Connecticut**

## Trade Show Tips

On February 28, the library and the Newington Chamber of Commerce co-sponsored the program How to Make the Most of a Trade Show. If you missed it, here are some useful hints from the presenter, Ron Failbusch, a trade exhibitor veteran.

* Buy a piece of carpet approximately 8' X 10'. It will fit the booths at most trade shows.

* Make your booth look inviting and interesting. Don't put barricades (like tables) between yourself and your potential customers.

* A flexible sign which can be rolled up is much easier to transport than an inflexible one. But you'll also want a durable sign that you can use over and over again.

* Don't bring a chair. If you sit at your booth people will be reluctant to "bother" you. Don't eat or read while in the booth.

* Make a checklist. Write down everything you'll need while at a trade show. Include everything from aspirin to Scotch tape to business cards. Mark items off as you pack them for the show.

* Promotional items are usually a waste of money. Think twice before you invest in doing this.

* Follow up quickly on any leads.

## Before You Buy . . .

The March issue of *What to Buy for Business* includes a special report on overnight and two-day letter/small packet deliveries. Check it out if you're wondering who delivers the best value.

The library's telephone number is 665-8700. Program it into your speed dial and use it often.

* Evaluation of business phone systems
* Preparation for real estate examinations
* Small business insurance plans
* Florida building codes
* How to register a trademark
* How to do real estate searches

Library staff has provided information on the following subjects:

## Have you called lately?

Librarians answer thousands of questions each year for businesses just like yours.

**Tip:**

*Do you know employees who need to improve their English speaking skills?* The library has an extensive collection of *audiocassettes for this purpose.*

## Personal Matters

Do you know the library has job descriptions of all types available for your business? Thousands of jobs are included in the *Dictionary of Occupational Titles.*

You can also find Connecticut salary and benefit information in *What to Do About Personnel Problems.* The figures are based on surveys conducted throughout the state.

## Holiday time . . .

means you have less time. Let the library staff help you keep the holiday stress to a minimum. Call the library for:

* addresses for entertainers
* recipes for your office party
* etiquette rules for gift giving

Gifts for employees are also available:

* a pen and ink print of the library for an office wall
* library notecards
* canvas book bags

*"My time with the business counselor at the library was very well spent. She helped me to brainstorm ideas and gave me an assignment that I had to complete in three weeks. It was a great motivator to take action on ideas I had for quite a while."*

top the list. Locations of parks and other recreation facilities could also be included. (Don't forget information on the library!) Mail one reproducible copy of the packet to businesses that are large enough to warrant it, and watch for announcements of expansions of the workforce or relocations of whole businesses.

## JOB AND CAREER INFORMATION

Job seekers come to the library for career information, sample test books, annual reports, and company profiles. With changes in the economy, many businesses are streamlining operations and retraining existing staff. Others provide postemployment counseling to those downsized out of a job. The library may have on hand more support materials for job seekers than do all but the very largest companies. This is the perfect time to let such companies know what you have and how you could lend it to them.

## BOOKLISTS

Beware!! This is the most common first step a library takes when introducing a service to the community, and it is *the least useful*. The message a booklist carries to the business person is, "These are the books we have for you to read or use." Yet, since time is the business person's most precious commodity, the perception that library use requires a major time commitment will quickly repel potential customers.

A booklist is most effective when it accompanies a program as a handout; its purpose can be explained and its titles are relevant to the topic at hand (see Figures 6–4, 6–5). Some libraries have found that a collection of typical or actual business questions together with the reference sources used to provide the answers is a useful alternative to the booklist (Figures 6–6, 6–7).

# Big Help for Small Business

O ne of the great recurring dreams for many Americans is to be their own boss, totally independent. The entrepreneurial spirit is as American as freedom and patriotism. In the last decade, small business start-ups by entrepreneurs have increased by 50 percent. Obviously, many people – young and old, male and female, white and minority – have worked hard to become independent small-business owners.

Courageous, self-reliant, patient, persistent, and energetic – these are just a few of the qualities entrepreneurs need. But they also must have knowledge and information. The fact is that 50 percent of all new business ventures fail within three years. Experts agree that these failures are most frequently caused by lack of information about the competition and the market, and by ignorance about the legal and financial aspects of running a business. Fortunately, Milwaukee Public Library can offer a wealth of information on all of these aspects of starting a small business.

**FIGURE 6–4  Cover Page of Business Booklist Brochure, Milwaukee, Wisconsin**

**FIGURE 6–5   Business Booklist, London, Ontario**

# Bookkeeping and Record Keeping for the Small Business

97.2 3 5

**Resources at
London Public Library**

Circulating Books

These books may be borrowed. Ask to reserve any book not on the shelf.

| | | |
|---|---|---|
| 657.2<br>D988pr | Dyer, Mary Lee<br>Practical Bookkeeping for the<br>Small Business | 1976 |
| 657.2<br>Fie | Fields, Louis<br>Bookkeeping Made Simple | 1990 |
| 657.2<br>Kra | Kravitz, Wallace W.<br>Bookkeeping the Easy Way | 1990 |
| 657.2<br>Pin | Pinson, Linda<br>Recordkeeping:  The Secret to<br>Profit and Growth | 1988 |
| 657.2<br>Rag | Ragan, Robert C.<br>Step-By-Step Bookkeeping | 1984 |
| 657.2<br>1987 | Ontario Small Business<br>Branch<br>Record Keeping Made Easy:<br>A Practical Bookkeeping and<br>Budgeting System for Your<br>New Small Business | 1987 |

95-153

## PERSONAL COMPUTER USE

Unlikely though it seems, some businesses have not computerized. Communal use of computers and printers is a service that libraries can offer to businesses as well as to the general public. Some items to consider are:

- laser printers
- color printers
- scanners
- desktop publishing software
- clip art on disk
- commonly used office software to sample before purchase

## BUSINESS COUNSELING

Together with the Small Business Administration, the Newington, Connecticut, library has business counseling sessions every week. Counselors from the Service Corps of Retired Executives (SCORE) and the Connecticut Small Business Development Centers (SBDC)conduct the sessions. The service is advertised in the local newspapers, in the Chamber of Commerce newsletter, the library's business newsletter, and on signs in the library's business section. The counselors are familiar with the library's goals in serving businesses, and they understand that much of the information they will recommend that their clients use is available in the library. At the end of a session, the business counselor can take the client to the information desk, introduce the client to the librarian, and explain what information is needed. To the client, the meeting becomes one-stop shopping.

Sessions last about ninety minutes. Scheduling is done by the library's information desk. On the day before the appointments, counselors get the names and phone numbers of the clients and call them for a preliminary discussion so as to prepare appropriate information.

FIGURE 6–6 Sample Business Booklist, London, Ontario

## London Public Library Means Business

**Do you have a question?
We'll help you find the answer.
That's OUR business.**

We've helped Londoners who asked:

✔ What is the address of GenTech? I don't know what they do or where they are, but I think it's in Canada somewhere.
*Canadian Key Business Directory*

✔ Is there a Canadian supplier for titanium dioxide?
*computer database*

✔ Which are the best performing mutual funds in Canada?
*Financial Post Survey of Funds*

✔ Can I get a list of American automobile auctioneers?
*Directories in Print*

✔ How do I find names of environmental consultants?
*Canadian Environmental Directory*

✔ A company named DuPont deMours was sold in 1914. Is there any way to find out who bought the company?
*Moody's Investors Service*

✔ What is the state of the welding industry in Ontario? How has free trade affected it?
*Canadian Index*

✔ How much money was lost to shoplifters last year?
*Shrinkage Survey of Canadian Retailers*

✔ My uncle in Europe wants information about barcoding.
*Prentice-Hall Encyclopedia of Information Technology*

✔ How do I set up a photography business?
*Library catalogue*

**You bring the questions.
We know where to find the answers.**

**Visit the business collection in East One -- on the east side of the main floor at the Central Library, 305 Queens Ave, 661-4600.**

*A LASTING TREASURE*
London Public Library since 1895

95-132

**FIGURE 6–7  Sample Business Booklist, Newington, Connecticut**

## An Information Specialist from the Reference Department will . . .

### take the question &

- What are some guidelines for controlling absenteeism?

- Where can I find a distributor of pressure gauges in Connecticut?

- What are the names and addresses of all the suppliers of business forms in the state?

- What is the franchise fee for Ben & Jerry's Homemade, Inc.?

- Is United Financial Casualty licensed in Connecticut?

- Where can I get a sample employee timesheet?

- Where can I find evaluations of fax machines?

- What radio station in Springfield, Massachussetts, will give me the greatest access to listeners 24-54 years of age?

### give the answer!

☑ *What to Do About Personnel Problems in Connecticut*

☑ *Regional Industrial Buying Guide for New England*

☑ *DIALOG on-line searching*

☑ *The Franchise Annual*

☑ *Best's Insurance Reports*

☑ *Business Forms on File*

☑ *What to Buy for Business*

☑ *Standard Rate and Data Service*

✓ = one of **many** information resources available

An Information Specialist is available during all library hours to answer your many questions. Either come in or call the library at 665-8700. The library strives to give your **business** the **personal** attention it needs.

## ENTREPRENEURIAL VENTURES

When library director Marcia Trotta of Meriden, Connecticut (population 57,000), returned from a trip to California, she mused about setting up a secondhand bookstore along the lines of the consignment shop she had just visited. When she approached the city manager with the idea, he offered a rent-free, city-owned, downtown, 1,500 square feet, corner property that was vacant at a time when the vacancy rate in the downtown area was a troublesome issue. One month later, furnished with excess library shelving and staffed by volunteers, a secondhand bookstore opened.

Sales in the first month averaged $120 a day. All profits go directly to the library, which has assumed responsibility for the operation's utility and telephone bills. A coin-operated copy machine is installed. Library officials have begun to add works by local authors, books in Spanish, and other items such as library book bags and stationery. The sale of refreshments is being explored. The store is open from 10 A.M. to 4 P.M. daily. The location, across the street from the police station and court house and a quarter-mile from the library, assures a steady stream of customers.

The project is a perfect example of the library helping to boost the economy, revitalize a downtown area, and market its services to a potential library clientele. City officials, citing the project's success and recognizing the library's role, have renewed commitment to library services through increased capital improvement funding.

## MAJOR EVENT COORDINATOR

In addition to the bookstore, the public library in Meriden ran a "First Night" event for the city. A booming downtown in the 1950s and '60s, Meriden came alive on Friday night for young and old alike—until malls drew people away. To help revive the downtown, the Meriden public library started "First Night" in 1993 to celebrate ninety years of library service. Seven buildings in the area adjacent to the library housed musical events and entertainment, with a shuttle bus available. Entry to all events cost $5 for adults and $1 for children. The first year, approximately 700 people attended; two years later, the event had expanded to fifteen locations with attendance of well over 1,000.

The library realized a twofold dividend from this venture. First, city government and residents alike now recognize the library as the major player in cultural activities in the city. Second, the library has proven the naysayers wrong in their claim that the downtown would never be alive again. In fact, many people's perception of the downtown has changed, and the entire area, including the library, has benefited because people are no longer afraid to come use the facilities.

# A NOTARY PUBLIC ON STAFF

At a recent program for real estate agents on the resources of the Newington, Connecticut, library, the resource receiving the most audible sounds of approval was the presence of a notary public on the library staff! This service costs the library very little per year in terms of registration fees and staff time for training and certification. Business people often need items notarized at hours when other establishments such as banks and town clerks offices are not open. This service alone can entice business people into the library for the first time. Once they do come in, you have the opportunity to offer a tour and any informational material you have on the library's business resources.

# TAX ASSISTANCE

Inquire at your local IRS office about having a tax expert for small businesses stationed in the library from January to April. Then offer to book appointments and advertise the service to the business community. Again, it's another opportunity to talk to people who may not have been in the library before and to introduce them to other services. The presence of a professional tax resource also relieves the reference staff from having to deal with patrons' tax questions.

# AGENCIES THAT CAN ASSIST, OR, YOU'RE NOT ALONE

Librarians are well versed in the act of referral. However, before referring any business patron to the local resources listed below, it is recommended that you visit the facilities if possible, talk to the service providers, and get a sense of their service delivery methods. A good referral is at least as valuable as a correctly answered reference question on the spot—and sometimes more so.

## NATIONAL AGENCIES

American Economic Development Council (AEDC)
9801 West Higgins Road, Suite 540
Rosemont, Illinois 60018
847-692-9944

Offers continuing education in industrial and economic development in university settings throughout the United States as well as on-site company training. Provides information on industrial and economic development and maintains a job placement service. Produces quarterly journal and a "practicing economic development" booklet. Holds an annual conference. Offers twenty courses at universities throughout the United States.

Corporation for Enterprise Development (CFED)
777 N. Capitol Street, NE, Suite 801
Washington, DC 20003
202-408-9788

Provides assistance to public and private organizations concerned with increasing the economic opportunity of individuals through the encouragement and support of enterprise development; serves as a forum for the exchange of ideas. Is devoted to the research, development, and dissemination of entrepreneurial policy initiatives at the local, state, and federal levels. Publishes *The Development Report Card for the States* (annual) and *The Entrepreneurial Review* (four times each year).

National Congress for Community Economic Development
1875 Connecticut Avenue, NW, Suite 524
Washington, DC 20009
202-234-5009

Provides a national program of promotion, partnership, and assistance for organizations in community-based economic development; monitors legislative issues. Provides start-up assistance to newly formed community-based economic development organizations. Sponsors information center and placement service. Compiles information on new programs in community economic development. Produces publications and holds semiannual conference.

National Council for Urban Economic Development (CUED)
1730 K Street, NW, Suite 915
Washington, DC 20006
202-223-4735

Works for public and private participants in global economic development. Provides information on job creation, attraction, and retention to members in order to build local economies. Gives Economic Development Award, Economic Leadership Award and others. Publishes quarterly journal; semimonthly newsletter and reports. Holds annual technical conference.

Service Corps of Retired Executives (SCORE)
409 Third Street, SW, Suite 5900
Washington, DC 20024
202-205-6762

A volunteer program sponsored by the Small Business Administration in which active and retired business people provide free management assistance to men and women who are considering starting a small business, encountering problems with their current one, or expanding.

Small Business Administration
(see agencies below that are affiliated with this department)

## STATEWIDE RESOURCES

### Small Business Development Centers

Mandated by Congress, these centers represent a partnership between the Small Business Administration, state universities, and the private sector. They provide one-on-one counseling as well as group training programs at locations around a state.

The centers can be consulted on all areas, including preventure feasibility, business plans, marketing, record keeping, financial planning, production, and preparation of financial documentation for loan packaging.

Services are provided by full-time professional business consultants along with faculty of the state university. All counseling and information services are free. Small fees are charged for most workshops, seminars and courses.

### Research Centers or Small Business Institutes

Check the *Small Business Sourcebook* for a listing of research centers in your state. Frequently these are set up within universities to assist entrepreneurs and provide training and formal courses. Sometimes they provide counseling, information, and support to small business people.

### State Departments of Economic Development

Usually located in a state's capital city, these agencies are responsible for the economic well-being of the state in terms of business growth and expansion. Much effort is put into retaining companies and enticing new businesses to settle. Contact them for loan programs, information on having a business in the state, and on working with other businesses in the state.

## Community Colleges

This is a low-cost alternative to four-year colleges for the small business person or the librarian who wants to learn about the business world. Often they are taught by adjunct faculty who have field experience during the day. Contacting teachers about library resources would benefit enrollees and the faculty.

## Service Corps of Retired Executives (SCORE)

There are many local branches of this national organization (see national section).

## Research and Technology Parks

These are science parks where tenants can interface with university research resources. They are sometimes referred to as technology transfer centers where newly tested technology is "transferred" from the university to the business sector. These are invaluable sources for technical advice, information, and networking. Check the *Small Business Sourcebook* for locations by state.

## LOCAL RESOURCES

## Utilities

The authorities that supply water, electricity, sewer services, fuel, cable television, and telephone service may have gathered important demographic information that can help local businesses. Often they have developed geographic information systems (GIS) in order to map the area that they serve—information that may potentially be available to the public library.

## Community Professionals

There are business people throughout your area who can prove to be valuable resources for you. Try contacting:

- bankers—for loan information, book values of automobiles, and amortization schedules
- property developers—for plans for property
- real estate agents—for advice in selecting property, appraisals, and available land
- attorneys—for legal advice in setting up a business
- accountants—for tax information, bookkeeping practices, and related software information
- municipal/county staff—from economic development officers to building inspectors and zoning officers, these are the people to partner with in your local community.

There may be local or regional economic development agencies in your area. Contact your state department of economic development for more information.

Universities may have developed services that could also be helpful. One example of this is MLINK, at the University of Michigan, which provides in-depth research services to governments, businesses, and community organizations in the areas of community and economic development. These services are provided only through the public libraries of Michigan. The purpose of the project is to promote the public library as a resource for economic development. To subscribe to MLINK's supporting listserv, send an e-mail message to: majordomo@mlink.hh.lib.umich.edu. Leave the subject line blank. In the body of your message type: Subscribe Michlib-l [your e-mail address]. Note: the last character of Michlib-l is a lower-case L.

# MARKETING

You have convinced the Chamber of Commerce and related agencies that you have a viable product to offer. You have trained your staff in the language of business. You have rewritten policies to accommodate the new customer. So now, you can just sit back and wait for an increase in business questions, confident that your answers will be better than ever, right? Wrong!

The major message that business focus groups have delivered to libraries throughout the country is that businesses need to be introduced to new library services the way they learn about any other service—*by a person they know and trust*. How to earn that trust? First and foremost, by having confidence in your product. Certainly, the sales calls can be effective, but they won't do you any good if you don't believe in what you're selling.

In a sales call, you are competing for someone's attention. Let's face it—when you have someone at the library's reference desk or on the telephone, they've already chosen your service. But now you're embarking into competitive territory. And the competition will be for the "buyer's" time as opposed to a concrete product. This chapter looks at several approaches used by libraries to bring the attention of the business community to the services they offer.

## THE PRESS

Focus groups have revealed that the tried-and-true approach of press releases in local editions of newspapers rarely yield results, because most business people read the newspaper at home, and most do not live and work in the same newspaper area. Instead, send releases to local business journals, the business page of the newspaper, and business and industry associations. If local organizations such as the Chamber of Commerce or Rotary Club have newsletters, send them information as well. Remember to provide news about staff promotions, elections to association offices, training courses completed, and awards. Business people read these pages. It is free publicity and helps get you viewed as a business entity.

Watch for opportunities in the press to respond. One alert staff member noticed a restaurant owner had written to his local food column about a recipe. The staffer found several variations on the recipe and mailed them to him. He thanked her in the ensuing column, for good results all around.

Send letters to the editor written over your own or the appropriate person's name (with permission, of course!) on any issue you feel needs raising. Have op-ed pieces ready for occasions that need promoting.

## THE AIRWAVES

Business people spend a considerable amount of time in their cars. Send radio spots to the stations that business people listen to. Get in touch with local radio stations that have talk shows and let them know that you are available for interviews. Encourage their research staff to call the show for information and ask in return that they mention their source of information on the air.

There may be a broadcasting school near you. See if they would lend a hand to produce a radio spot that could be used as a public service or as a paid spot. It will add to the student's resume, teach the student about library services, and reach new listeners.

## CYBERSPACE

Cyberspace, or the Internet, is an inexpensive way to promote the public library. Think of this new medium as the newspaper or radio, and do what you might do with each of those. For instance, you read the news, figure out how it applies to you, and act on it. The same approach works with the Internet. Find out what newsgroups or mailing lists businesses use. Note their concerns, and respond, as appropriate, to either the entire list or the individual.

You can also advertise your library's services through an Internet home page. Be sure that it highlights your services to businesses. If your community also has a presence on the Internet, ask for links from the business sections to your business section.

# DIRECT MAIL

Direct mail is tricky. Your piece must be impressive enough not to land in the circular file. An advance postcard announcing an important mailing may help, since postcards do not need to be opened. Try to use the same color and logo on the postcard that you will use on the following mailing, so that it is recognized and opened. Do not send the postcard out more than a week before the mailing or it will long be forgotten.

Mail something useful rather than promotional. For example, the children's department at the Newington, Connecticut, library produced an annotated list of children's books and resources for dealing with death and dying. These were sent in bulk to local funeral homes, veterinarians (the list addressed the death of pets), and hospitals. (Due to the expense, the institutions were called ahead of time to make sure that such a package would be welcome.) Follow-up calls found that most funeral homes added the material to the packet of information given to families with children, veterinarians placed them in waiting rooms, and social workers in hospitals and nursing homes gave them to families in need.

To supplement a program for real estate agents, the Newington library staff prepared a list of resources for the mover, the buyer, and the seller (see Figure 7–1). Copies were sent to those who attended the session as well as those that did not, and in sufficient supply for all their anticipated clients that coming year. A follow-up call by library staff regarding the brochure reacquainted the agency with the library's services.

A brochure of topical resources might not be seen as an economic development project. The key is to remember the economic development angle each time you deal with a business and offer other information services. For instance, should any funeral home be without a directory like the *Encyclopedia of Associations* for memorial donation designations? Perhaps such a business would be interested in purchasing last year's edition at a reduced cost. A call to offer something is an opportunity to market other services.

## USING DIRECT MAIL TO OFFER A SERVICE

Mail out a specific service offer, such as the availability of meeting room space. While providing meeting facilities is not a library's main thrust, acceptance of the offer will provide you with an opening into their business. If you decide to market this aspect, remind the staff member who books your meeting rooms of the

**FIGURE 7–1** Cover of Brochure for Real Estate Agents

# THE BUSINESS OF REAL ESTATE

Information to assist you and your customers . . . .

Lucy Robbins Welles Library
95 Cedar Street
Newington, CT 06111
voice: (203) 665-8700
fax: (203) 667-1255
modem (to connect to library catalogs): (203) 665-7312

importance of the business presence in the library and accommodating the users' requirements. Businesses may ask for supplies and amenities such as they find at conference centers: be prepared for requests for pitchers of water, laser pointers, flip charts, and coffee service. If your budget is tight, have alternatives ready such as a referral to a commercial service that could provide these items.

The staff member who serves the business community should know when a business group will be meeting in the library so that he or she can greet participants at the door. Business gatherings offer the opportunity for a formal welcome, a concise description of library business services, and a tour at the break.

## USING DIRECT MAIL TO DISSEMINATE NEWSLETTERS

Newsletters targeted to the business community can be effective places to advertise your efforts with other businesses. Within that newsletter, mention the business connections you have made during the month, and include thank-you notes to businesses for their gifts toward programs or similar contributions. Such items plant a seed in other minds to do the same thing and provide advertising of the best kind for the business that has assisted you—far more effective than the thank-you letter seen by only one person.

# AWARDS CEREMONIES

Awards call attention to an organization's mission and honor exceptional contributions. Whether the gift is the donation of a major reference work or funding for a concert series, a formal public acknowledgment strengthens the relationship between the donor and the library. Schedule the award ceremony to emphasize the recipient's corporate importance. The presentation could coincide with a concert the award recipient sponsored or the annual meeting of your library. Give a framed print of the library as a tangible token; when it is displayed at the business premises, it advertises the library and reminds that business's employees about the library's importance.

Local Chambers of Commerce often give annual awards. If you are an active member of the chamber, volunteer for the awards committee. The participation will give you insight into businesses that provide valuable services and will help educate other committee members about contributions businesses make to the library. Offer to present one of the awards and demonstrate your own public-speaking skills. If you receive an award, capitalize on the opportunity. Send a press release to those who helped you to receive it and thank those people in your acceptance speech. Often these awards ceremonies are broadcast on local-access television and can draw a large live audience.

## MEETINGS

Attending meetings and gatherings of business people is critical. Make sure the library budget allows for such expenses. But do not make the fatal mistake of sticking close to those you know. Circulate and, if there is more than one of you from the library, spread out to work the crowd; you can talk to each other later. By spreading out, you can meet that many more people and advertise your product. If a staff member doesn't have the confidence to face sitting with strangers at a gathering, send him or her the first time with someone who can model appropriate behavior. If the staffer still does not want to tackle it, find someone else.

At one Chamber of Commerce meeting, a librarian sat with a group of people whom she didn't know. Within this group she met a telecommunications expert who worked for the local telephone company. He later became a member of the library board and has been an advocate for pricing differentials for libraries and a source of in-kind contributions ever since!

Business meetings often begin at 7:30 A.M. or 5 P.M. Be flexible enough to rearrange schedules to permit a staff member to attend. The time spent out of the building is often more valuable than several hours inside talking to repeat customers.

## TRADE SHOWS

A trade show quickly places you in front of different segments of the marketplace—both those who stop and those who exhibit. A local business showcase is a good starting point both in terms of reaching potential customers in your geographical area and preparing for similar events of a larger scope.

A trade show can be grueling, and doing one effectively requires, among other things, stamina. However, librarians have an advantage here, since they have experience in answering questions of every kind all day long at the reference desk.

Your display should draw people in, so contact a company that specializes in trade show displays to have one constructed professionally. The display board should be compact enough to carry easily and should not require electricity; renting electrical outlets can be very expensive, and you do not want to have to choose between an illuminated sign and a computer demonstration. The display should call attention to the message you want to convey to attendees. The exhibit itself could combine a demonstration of a particular service, such as information retrieval capabilities, along with handout materials like brochures and business cards for those passing by.

Tips from people who work the trade shows are:

- Bring a carpet square to stand on—it makes it easier on the feet.
- Dress comfortably, but appropriately, for the crowd.
- Never stand behind a booth. Always be out and about.
- Know your crowd.
- Look at name tags and relate quickly to the name, the company, or the product, or else you could lose them.
- Believe in what you're selling.
- Send two people, so that each can get a break and visit other booths. This time can also provide valuable contacts.

## PERSONAL CONTACTS

Word-of-mouth is very powerful advertising, but people have to know you and your services in order to mention you to others, so get yourself known. Have lunch or breakfast in places popular with the business crowd. Patronize local businesses. Let them know who you are and what the library can do for them. Business people who deal primarily with other business people as opposed to the general public are important contacts. Pay particular attention to printers, public relations companies, quick copy businesses, and answering services.

Target educators who specialize in business matters and keep them up-to-date on your facilities and services. One financial planner who taught classes in a local adult education program told her class not to bother going to the local library because it did not have a certain investment service. It turned out the library had in fact been subscribing to the service for several months but had never thought to let that person know.

Adult education programs often include classes on starting a business. Provide whoever is teaching the classes with an inventory of relevant materials available at the library. Offer to hold one of the classes at the library so that students can be introduced to the resources. Talk to the teachers of English as a second language. These classes often include people who are both learning English and thinking about starting a business similar to one they may have had in another country. Think creatively about developing contacts.

Remember that real estate brochure sent by direct mail? Even better than the postal service is a staff visit to the business to drop off a brochure. This type of trip may sound time consuming, because key people may not be in the office. But even if your contact at this point is the office manager, remember that this is the person who probably answers the phone and opens the mail—the first line of defense you have to break through!

## PROGRAMS

Libraries are always offering special programs, but programming for the business community presents a challenge. The business owner has to be convinced that the experience will be worth the loss of production when an employee is out of work for a day. Even though library focus groups repeatedly identified the need for courses in such topics as time management and diversity, too few signed up for the programs, so they were cancelled. Why the low turn-out? Either the time wasn't right, the decision maker never saw the flier, or the event was considered inexpedient when compared to the real-life challenge of keeping the small business afloat.

However, when you plan a business program successfully, the library scores. To bolster interest, visibility, and enrollments, you can team up with another agency such as the Small Business Development Center, SCORE, your municipality's economic development department, or the Chamber of Commerce. Often an organization will be happy to lend its name, and its sponsorship gives credence to your advertising, but it leaves you still in charge of the content of event.

To charge or not to charge? A price adds value, and the fee can be an incentive for attendance if prepaid. Businesses are used to being charged for services, but libraries often feel that they want to reach the people who can afford it the least. Some ways to solve this dilemma include:

- Charge for materials (it doesn't quite sound the same as charging for the program).
- Have the sponsoring agency collect the money and send the library a percentage.
- Charge certain people such as nonresidents or walk ins.

It's a difficult decision to make no matter which direction you take.

There are several issues to consider when planning a program for businesses.

## THE TOPIC

It has to be timely, critical, and close to home. Choose based on what you know of your community, what its needs are. Topics that will draw good crowds in general are how to write a marketing plan, how to work a trade show, how to select a computer for your business, and employee practices related to areas such as the Americans with Disabilities Act, diversity, and sexual harassment.

## THE TIME

Survey your audience before setting a time. Don't expect them to give up an entire day; that is just too much time. Try to schedule the event outside normal business hours. If you are targeting a group that cannot leave their stores, for instance, try an early evening starting time and offer a light dinner.

## THE TARGET AUDIENCE

Unless you have a topic that is brand new to the business world such as the Internet, you have to target the audience. No one has time to be in the wrong workshop. Time is money and, unlike those who attend gardening or travel programs, this audience isn't using its leisure time. Describe as clearly as possible who should attend and why. Have some potential participants read the description and ask them if they can tell from the write-up if they should attend or not. *Describe the benefits*, not the features, of the program.

## THE SIGN-UP

Use direct sales. Just as librarians have an audience in mind when they select books, you should have someone in mind when you plan the program. Make sure there is interest before planning the program, then personally invite the participants. This approach may require a telephone call, a personal note, or even a visit.

## THE LOCATION

Is the purpose to get them into the library or to get them to know about and use library resources as a result of what they have learned? The answer is hopefully the latter. If so, the location doesn't matter. If members of the target audience frequent a certain room in a restaurant, have it there. If a suitable conference room in a local business is available, go there.

### The In-house Audience

This could be one of your best solutions. Talk to a company that regularly offers in-house training and get a sense of what you could offer. If the employees are required to attend and do not have to change their pattern, they will be there. They might not be your most enthusiastic crowd (at first, anyway), but you'll have them captive and be able to sell your services.

### THE REMINDER

You've got the right number signed up. The day comes and only 25 percent show up. What happened? First of all, no-shows are far more common in the business world than among other audiences. Again, unlike our personal lives, our business lives are governed by someone else. Because of that constraint, you must work to get as many people as possible to follow through on their reservation. Make telephone calls the day before if that is possible. The direct, personal approach might assure the attendance of people who are wavering.

---

*Warning! No matter how popular the programs you have for the general public are, that does not mean business programs will be also. The "book it and they will come" theory doesn't work with businesses.*

## Programs that Work

### Secretary's Day training

Often the person lowest in the office pecking order is the one central to the operation. Take advantage of Secretary's Day or Week to offer a continuing education program for the secretary. Include all the resources libraries have that help answer questions secretaries are asked—everything from where to buy fax machine paper to how to write a letter of recommendation. One secretary told library staff that the library is her secret weapon: the people at her company think she's brilliant because she can always come up with the answer, but it's really the library's reference staff that does the work! You can bet that she opens all the letters from the library and reads the business newsletter carefully.

### Real estate agents

Real estate agents are often the first and maybe the last people that people outside the community have contact with. The more agents know about the community, the more impressed their clients will be. Real estate agents need to know the answers to such diverse questions as comparative property taxes among towns, schools' per-pupil spending, and meeting dates of the Rotary Club. Because the library can be one of the prime selling points in the community, encourage agents to take prospective homeowners into the library. Agents also deal with people leaving the community, and it will benefit them to know what information you have on other locations. It is also a great time to tout that garage sale video and the books on how to pack right.

### Beauty salon personnel

Hair stylists, manicurists, and cosmetologists have people in your community captive for hours every month. They can not only benefit from knowing what the library has on purchasing, customer service, marketing, and displays, but can also be a talking advertisement while they perform their work.

### Journalists

While reporters from the large media organizations have in-house research departments, their counterparts from smaller newspapers and television and radio stations do not. This latter segment is tailor-made for library services, with its needs for prompt, accurate information and knowledge of potential local advertisers. In return, you might find reporters supporting your position in their coverage of local controversial issues such as censorship or budget referenda.

## Internet neophytes

Librarians know how much they *don't* know about the Internet, but in general, they know a quantum leap more than the general public. Just read the trade journals of other organizations; with the exception of the computer world, articles about the Internet aren't flooding the tables of contents. You get the advertisements each week for courses given throughout the country on using the Internet. Just follow their outline and arrange for a Net demonstration, using computer projection for a large crowd or a very big monitor for a smaller group. The audience will be impressed. But don't be surprised if the questions still center on the best modem to buy and the differences between the Internet service providers and the commercial services.

## THREE BUSINESS PROGRAM EXPERIENCES

### Glendale, Arizona

The Glendale, Arizona(population 160,000), library recently changed the frequency of its business programs from monthly to weekly. The dedication of the staff, an enthusiastic audience, and an abundance of excellent program presenters were factors behind this step. Topics that have proved particularly popular include:

- small business and the law
- women and career changes
- how to buy a computer for a home office
- how to write a business plan: for women only

Programs start at a variety of times, ranging from 7 A.M. to 2 P.M. to evenings. Although preregistration is required, some people who sign up do not show, and some people who do not sign up do show! A limited budget discontinued the practice of offering refreshments. However, this change did not affect the generally positive evaluations of the audience.

### Milwaukee Public Library

The Milwaukee Public Library needed a new way to reach the business community efficiently and economically. They decided to plan an early morning breakfast "wake-up" program. The library contacted the local weekly business newspaper to be the media sponsor and used newspaper personnel as the pilot group to try out the program.

Encouraged by the pilot group's reaction, the library initially ran a series of four weekly programs, but had to cut back to a monthly schedule because of staffing and budgetary limitations. The library staff sent announcements to the city's list of businesses plus those on a mailing list from the SCORE office, and ran large ads in the newspaper. An average of fifty people registered and forty attended each event. One-third registered because of the ad (Figure 7–2), one-third because of the mailing (Figure 7–3), and one-third because of in-house publicity. Both the publisher of the sponsoring newspaper and the city librarian opened each session with welcoming remarks. The participants then divided into smaller groups for introductions to various areas in the library.

The Milwaukee Public Library declared the program series a success. Two hundred people were introduced to the services each month. Their media sponsor donated $7,000 worth of advertising. Librarians worked at introducing *themselves* as well as the resources to the participants. And most important, people came back to work with the resources after seeing them on the tour.

### Rolling Meadows, Illinois

An annual event at the Rolling Meadows library has been the InfoFair. Business people are invited for an 8 A.M. continental breakfast and a showcase of business-related information sources. Librarians divide up resources into various areas such as their on-line catalog system, CD-ROM local area network area, print resources, and a staff area where on-line searching takes place. Librarians at Rolling Meadows are careful to emphasize that they are the main resources and that they simply use the tools to demonstrate how they find answers. They do not want to create the impression that a business person has to know how to search and negotiate the various databases.

## DIRECT SALES

The most repeated comment by librarians who were asked about their work with the business community was, "I wish we could get out of the library and talk to them directly."

You can! Children's departments have known for years that they have to go where the children are—parks, day-care centers, schools. Adult services staff often find themselves at nursing homes promoting books. Why shouldn't librarians serving the business community go to where their potential customers are?

Some librarians are delighted to be asked to address the local

**FIGURE 7–2   Advertisement for "Wake-Up" Program**

# "Wake-up" to library resources for business.

**FREE**
**Library Resources for Business**
**"Wake-Up" Seminar**

**7:30 - 8:45 A.M.**
Central Library - 814 W. Wisconsin Ave.

**Dates Include:**
November 10, 1994
November 17, 1994
December  1, 1994
December  8, 1994

There's a lot of information out there to help you in your business... and the library's trained specialists can save you time in getting what you need. Learn more about the QUICK, VALUABLE INFORMATION the library can offer. Come meet your research specialists. Find out how they can help you succeed... the rewards could be endless.

Add a specialized library to your small business for client research... mailing list development... trademark searching... state-of-the-art technology... you name it ... come to one of these free seminars and find out how our specialists can help. To register call 286-3031. Advanced registration is recommended and space is limited.

Sponsored by:

The Business Journal

MILWAUKEE
PUBLIC
LIBRARY

**FIGURE 7–3    Brochure for "Wake-Up" Program**

**Welcome to the
Wake-Up Seminar
Sponsored by**

**The
Business
Journal**
*Your local business
news authority.*

MILWAUKEE
PUBLIC
LIBRARY

**Presenting Library Resources
for Business**

**7:30 a.m. Welcome**

Kathleen M. Huston, City Librarian

Mark J. Sabljak, publisher, The Business Journal

Sandra Lockett, Assistant City Librarian for Central
Library Services

**7:45 a.m. Tour
Periodicals Service Area**

Government documents, Newspapers, Periodicals and
TAP file
CD-ROM Resources
 ProQuest (ABI Inform, Periodicals Index,
  Newspaper Index)
 Government Documents (Marcive GPO CAT/PAC
  Plus, Government Periodicals Index)
        Periodicals Coordinator: Dawn Lauber

**Humanities Service Area**
(Law and History)

CD-ROM Resources
 Phone Disc
 Biography and Genealogy Master Index
 Encyclopedia of Associations
 United States Code
 Wislaw (Wisconsin Statutes, etc.)
        Humanities Coordinator: Virginia Schwartz

**Business and Technology Service Area**

*Business* (Small Business Resources, Marketing,
 Foreign and Domestic Trade)
CD-ROM Resources
 National Trade Data Bank
 '90 Federal Census of WI
 '90 U.S. Census Summary
 InfoTrac-Health Reference Center
 InfoTrac-Business Collection
 Dun's Business Locator
 Statistical MASTERFILE
 American Business Disc
        Business Librarian: Beverly DeWeese

*Technology* (U.S. Patents, Trademark, Engineering and
 Industry Military Standards and Specifications)
CD-ROM resources
 APS-Automated Patent Search System
 CASSIS-Trademark Patents
 Worldwide Standards Index
 OSHA Regulations, Documents and Technical
  Information
Science, Business & Technology Coordinator: Beverly DeWeese

**8:30 a.m. Questions and Coffee**

business group. But any group presentation is just that—a general talk, where public speaking skills count for more than specific knowledge of resources. The environment of the group presentation, while a useful approach, maintains an invisible boundary between speaker and audience not unlike that between teacher and class. What's missing is the critical element of the one-on-one personal interaction on which many business people have come to rely. Focus groups repeatedly stress that the most effective way to introduce business people to a new product, service, or concept is through trust based on reputation and personal contact.

That attitude opens the door to direct sales by your staff—if they are backed by institutional support. A librarian who steps out of the building has to know that upon returning she will have the time, resources, and support of other staff members to get an answer back to the customer. To reiterate, calls from a new business patron who asks specifically for the liaison librarian must be handled professionally. Appointments by staff with business people must be honored, and reference desk time should accommodate these obligations.

The internal efforts pay off. Shirlee-Ann Kober, business specialist at the Newington library, has called on over fifty businesses in the past year. She feels that spending the time in their working environment puts the business person at ease, creates opportunities for to view how the workplace really operates, and makes a strong statement about the library's interest in the success of business.

## GETTING IN THE DOOR

To anyone in sales, the greatest challenge is getting face to face with the person he or she needs to speak to. A librarian should have a slight advantage, because no commercial product is being sold. But time—even to hear about *free* services—is an extremely valuable commodity for any business person. So how do you get the busy customer to see it's worthwhile spending time learning about library services?

1. Start with someone who already knows a bit about your services, someone that you know will be generally supportive.

2. Have her critique your visit and give recommendations for future ones.

3. Ask your first customer to be part of a feature story for your local business section or newsletter, then send copies to subsequent people to be visited.

4. Ask the first business to recommend other businesses and to call them to gain an entree for you.

Remember that most people are flattered at the thought of showing off their operation. Let them take you on a tour of the facility. Listen for clues about the operation and issues they are facing, new services they may be adding, or any new positions that are being created. Come prepared with as much background as you can on their industry in general and their business in particular; you'll be able to ask better, more informed questions. Take along some resources that every business seems to need—information about personnel management; business purchasing; and office computer information. Ask questions that can turn into questions for you to research. If the company is in the market for a new fax machine or is wondering about using a different delivery service, get some particulars and send some consumer information.

Once you've gotten your feet wet, you'll develop a routine. You might send an introductory letter to a business owner and enclose some literature and a business card. Promise to call in a few days to set up an appointment.

Warning! Your first calls may yield disappointment. The owner may be difficult to reach. He may not remember receiving your letter, and you may have to start from the beginning. The owner may misinterpret your intentions and either brush you off or insist that they don't need any. Your ego may take a bruising at this point.

Sometimes the person you meet initially will not be the one you need to reach. Ask to speak with the human resources person or purchasing agent if you believe you might make more headway with them. In a smaller situation, try including another partner or the office manager.

Some business people will welcome you but never let on that they can use your services. Indeed, they will try to impress you with how much they do not need outside assistance. That's okay. Just keep them in mind and send information their way whenever you think it is appropriate. You might be able to provide ancillary services such as meeting-room space, training programs, or audio-visual equipment for loan.

The other end of the spectrum is the business person you immediately click with. This one is anxious to hear what you have to offer, understands the value of information to her organization, and cannot believe she never thought of the library in the past. These are the business people who add a rewarding finish to personal calls.

As veteran salespeople know, the appointment technique for getting in the door does not always work. It may be necessary for the librarian to resort to the "cold call," i.e., walking in the door without any previous notification. If you and the library are known within the community already, this will not be as daunting as it sounds. Determine the best time of day for that particular business, know the names of the people you are trying to see, and go in with a positive manner. The cold call is especially effective in retail establishments.

# SERVICE DELIVERY

Some libraries may feel that their personnel and scheduling structures cannot absorb the extra work that the business community demands. Three libraries in particular faced such a situation. To respond, they changed their service delivery methods.

## THE FEE-BASED SERVICE

Johnson County, Kansas (population 300,000), is a rapidly growing metropolitan area. A highly educated community with a 50 percent library card registration brings in over 14,000 reference questions per month. There is tremendous support for library service as evidenced by a library construction bond issue that passed by an overwhelming margin in 1995.

Three-quarters of the local businesses are small, entrepreneurial types that use the library heavily. Between 30 and 40 percent of the reference questions Johnson County receives are business related. This usage level is due to the library's reputation for an excellent business collection and responsive service.

As the demand grew for more in-depth assistance and an expressed willingness to pay for the assistance, Johnson County responded by establishing JCL Research Plus. A fee-based service, JCL Research Plus offers a higher level of assistance to the patron who does not have the time or expertise to spend researching a particular feature. The public library had the foresight to see that "that someone" could be the library staff.

The library administration views the fee-based service as an option rather than a necessity to produce revenue. JCL managers realized that seeking information is not something most people do routinely in their jobs and that the learning curve is high, and that it makes sense for a small business person to contract out for information services above and beyond the customary answers that a reference librarian can normally supply in fifteen minutes.

Staff from the fee-based service work hand-in-hand with traditional reference staff. When a question comes to the JCL fee-based service that is really a ready reference matter, it is referred to the reference librarian. If a reference librarian detects that a patron wants more in-depth research, the fee-based service is offered. It is an option, not a way to avoid hard reference questions or to make money.

Between its start in March 1994 until February 1995, the service handled seventy-one projects at an average cost of $150 per project. The charge is based on an hourly fee of $60 and includes any on-line database expenses. The only advertising has been an article in the local newspaper and a listing in the telephone book.

However, Andreanna Kounas, Fee-Based Services Manager, is quick to point out that the meter doesn't start as soon as she picks up the phone. She first listens to the customer to determine if the question is truly a candidate for the fee-based services or one better handled at the reference desk. For example, a woman called wanting information on starting a business. Ms. Kounas referred her to resources in the community such as SBDC, SCORE, SBA, the county economic research department, and a new business incubator program. The inquiry was not a candidate for a fee-based service at that point. But because JCL Research Plus is advertised in the Yellow Pages and the library is not, people assume their business-related questions are candidates for the service. Therefore, the librarian needs to understand the level of depth the client wants and touches base after every level of searching to make sure the information is on target.

The public library ethic of looking until a question is answered permeates the fee-based service, but not to the detriment of the customer's pocketbook. The customer is getting personal service without the pressure of cost recovery as a direct goal. There's a difference.

Ms. Kounas attributes her ability to handle the demands of this service on her strong corporate library background, where the delivery of the information was key, as opposed to teaching someone to use a source or handing over many citations and expecting the patron to select what is applicable. Ms. Kounas believes librarians have to have an entrepreneurial spirit themselves and be risk takers in order to successfully provide information to business people. She finds two Internet mailing lists to be particularly helpful: FISCAL (fee-based information services in academic settings) and BUSLIB (for special and business librarians throughout the world).

The staffing for the service includes Ms. Kounas, who also works several hours each week on the reference desk, a non-MLS information specialist, and two other reference librarians assigned part-time to the service in addition to their regular duties. The budget for resources is mostly mixed in with the reference department budget with the exception of $3,000 for searching thesauri, a separate *Encyclopedia of Associations*, and other reference sources. The Johnson County library is looking forward to a LAN and a WAN (wide area network) that will allow the sharing of CD-ROM resources anywhere in the building.

Some examples of questions handled are:

- patent searches
- marketing information for small marketing and ad agencies
- surveys for businesses that want to launch a new product
- research on the types and costs of building materials that are used overseas
- job search information for people from outside the area

There is concern among Johnson County administrators about the perception of the fee-based service. If seen as a money-making arm of the library, the approach could result in negative public relations that would mean the denial of public money to support services and the library no longer being able to provide free basic services. This problem is dealt head-on by planned internal marketing among the staff and "tag team" presentations by fee-based services staff along with regular business reference staff to community and business groups. The two library units are seen as a team by people within the organization and potential customers and taxpayers.

## DOCUMENT DELIVERY

After four years of a fee-based service for business, library officials at the Milwaukee Public Library decided to discontinue it. While the demand and the income was growing each year, the library felt it could better utilize its greatest resource—the librarians—by putting them back "on the floor" with the general business questions. The bottom line is that each situation is different as to library staff, business community, and taxpayer—among other variables. No one style will fit any single institution. Milwaukee converted the fee-based reference service to a document delivery service, charging $5 for 20 pages or less and $3 for each additional 20 pages. They will fax businesses 10 pages for $2 (see Figure 7–4).

Milwaukee Public found that the library orientation did not lend itself to charging for services and that document delivery was a more clear-cut service that was easily differentiated from information delivery.

## REFERRAL SERVICES

The Carroll County, Maryland (population 130,000), library operates a unique lawyer referral service. The reference staff at Carroll County was aware of the need for legal assistance for business people as well as the general public. In a ground-breaking partnership, the library paired up with the Carroll County

**FIGURE 7–4** Advertisement for Document Delivery Service

Ditto

a copy service of the Milwaukee Public Library

**We'll copy it for you**

magazine articles • newspaper articles • patents
industry standards • military specifications
and many other materials copied in a timely fashion

**414-286-3065**

**Fill out request form on the back** of this brochure. Leave it with the librarian.

**or** **Fax it** 414-286-2126

**or**

**Your completed order can be picked up** at the Science Desk on the 2nd floor of Central Library or the drive-in window, 755 N. 8th St.

**We will gladly mail or fax it to you.**

**Prices per item**

COPY CHARGES - 20 pages or less — $5 (plus tax; postage included)

Each additional 20 pages — $3 (plus tax)

FAX CHARGES - every 10 pages — $2 (plus tax)

Additional charge for rush requests.

MILWAUKEE PUBLIC LIBRARY

Bar Association, to which the bar association provides attorneys and the library provides referral staff.

Attorneys pay an annual registration fee to the library in order to participate. When a client approaches the library for a referral, a librarian selects an attorney and places a conference call to the attorney's office so the library patron can schedule an appointment. The $25 charged for a thirty-minute consultation is collected by the attorney's office but returned to the library. If the client decides to retain the attorney, subsequent fees are set that do not include the library.

The referral service is housed at the library in a private, confidential office setting. During the first year of operation, 245 referrals were made for persons who had nowhere else to turn. Participants praised the excellent listening skills of the librarians, their ability to put facts together, and their sensitivity toward their problems. Costs to start the service were $1,000, and $4,400 was received from lawyer registration and referral fees, for a net profit of $3,400.

The implications for a business partnership modeled on Carroll County's general program are evident. While most people with established businesses have an attorney in place, those exploring options may need and appreciate such a service provided by the public library.

## OTHER OPTIONS

Other service delivery models that include fees could be:

1. the establishment of a support office staff for small businesses that need some assistance with telephone answering, word processing, mailing services, copying, faxing, e-mail retrieval, and the like

2. a center for trying out popular business software and computer equipment prior to purchasing

3. individual appointments with reference staff.

The age-old conflict about fee versus free for information services will not be solved easily nor have the same outcome in each community. When business people are accustomed to paying for services and they themselves are asking to be charged, it can be difficult to stand totally behind the free service delivery ethic. Each library governing authority should carefully examine the community's needs and make decisions and provisions accordingly.

# 3 RESULTS

There are a number of barometers by which to measure the success of a business reference service. Some can be quantified; others are measured by less tangible indicators.

## PROFESSIONAL SATISFACTION

In talking to business librarians throughout the country, one hears statements of satisfaction as a recurring theme:

The results I get when answering a business question fuel me for the next challenge. Unlike regular reference questions, I get closer to the customer. There's a real name and a real need attached to the question. I see the smiles and the satisfaction with an answer. It's almost a possessiveness—I'm answering a question for *my* customer, so I'd better do a great job. It's different from working a three-hour shift at the reference desk and walking away at the end of a shift.

It's a different constituency than the general public. I feel like I'm making a difference and establishing a professional relationship that will continue to grow.

I know the patron better, so I can make wiser purchases for the collection. There's less guessing and more purchased with a specific need in mind.

I get measurable satisfaction, more contact with the customer, repeated exposure to some of the same people, and the customer looks to me as their representative. It's a real boost.

This kind of job satisfaction generates high morale, a low absence rate, loyalty to the institution, few labor issues, and a generally all-around healthy institution.

# BUSINESS SATISFACTION

Business owners who use the library for information and have come to know and count on reference librarians as an arm of their operation are unstinting in their support. The owner of a public relations firm comments:

The services of the public library are equal to the time and knowledge I would have acquired in getting an MBA. I see it as self-education. It's equal to the value of a consultant. I feel that the reference librarians are part of my team without the overhead. It gives me a "virtual company."

Without the library, I would be spending money in bookstores, I'd have to hire an information specialist who might not care specifically about my business and the well-being of the town. I would have to work much harder at an area I'm not talented in. Now that I've found it, I can't imagine a business without the resources of the public library available to it.

A business management company's owner concurs:

The library has played an incredibly vital role in the growth and development of my business and continues to be a partner in its daily operations. Initially, I took pride in my researching skills while taking advantage of classes at the library in how to use new computerized resources. Quickly, however, I learned that the library's reference staff is comprised of invaluable information experts. They have experience in information retrieval and are able to maneuver among resources I am often unaware of . . . and they do so eagerly and with record-breaking speed. With their help, I've learned how to ask questions in a way that is meaningful to them and brings the results I am looking for.

By relying on these information professionals, I've become more efficient and effective as a business consultant and, ultimately, passed time and cost savings on to my clients.

Librarians have put me on the path to bar-coding companies, up-scale retailers in Canada, and calendar distribution channels in New England—and at no cost.

The information specialists at my library are easily the most valuable resource I can image having access to.

# TANGIBLE RESULTS

## NEW BUSINESS

"Librarian Books Rockwell International" is a headline usually reserved for dreams. But in the small town of Bellevue, Iowa (population 2,500), Marian Kieffer did just that—she landed a Fortune 500 company in her role as the town's librarian/economic development staff person!

Inspired by a talk given by another librarian, Kieffer and a library board member decided that it was very appropriate to get involved in economic development. What started out as assisting the Chamber of Commerce by writing promotional brochures and a community fact file resulted in Kieffer being asked by the City Council to serve as the economic development contact person for Bellevue. So Kieffer, a part-time employee, became the center of the community's activities for development as well as for its community education. The average day might bring an inquiry or two about leasing space or the town's permit requirements. However, one snowy day in January, two men in jeans and flannel shirts appeared without fanfare or introduction and insisted on meeting only with her and seeing available property.

There were many meetings in which the pair maintained their anonymity. Kieffer persuasively presented "quality of life" information such as student test scores, park facilities, and entertainment venues. She also assured them that a workforce was ready and able. Rockwell was looking at other locations in eastern Iowa as well, but the wealth of well-organized material helped sell them on Bellevue. The creation of two hundred fifty new jobs with good wages and benefits in a clean industry validated Bellevue's librarian/economic development director's new status.

## INCREASED FUNDING

Jeff Krull, director of the Allen County Public Library in Fort Wayne, Indiana (population 200,000), approached the pending legislative session with some anxiety about making a convincing pitch for funding. But thanks to a well-established business department (examples of which are scattered throughout this book), he only had to sit there. As he began to give testimony in defense of an increased millage, a legislator cut him off and touted the abilities of the library. Jeff knew enough to let the legislator carry the ball, and the proposal passed easily.

Yet, he warns, such success doesn't come overnight. It took about five years to win over key people in the community. Many were originally unacquainted with the library, so there was no base from which to start. Krull encourages librarians to view expert business services as a long-term investment, not to expect an immediate impact on funding, and to know that the service meets a very important community need.

## PRIDE

In Newington, Connecticut, a Town Council member by night and computer consultant by day was at a client's office in a nearby town. The client had an informational question beyond the consultant's expertise. Remembering that the Newington library welcomes questions from businesses, he encouraged the person to pick up the telephone and ask the question. What an opportunity! The person called the library, asked the question, and was given the answer within a minute. The Town Council member beamed with pride and, at the next budget hearing for the library, told the story and led the support for the library's request.

## USE OF BUSINESS RESOURCES

When business patrons go to great lengths to check with their best resource for information, that's a strong statement about your worth. In Southfield, Michigan, the library's reputation has grown to such a degree that patrons have called from planes for information: a business person on his way to Memphis called from the plane to get a list of health clubs near his hotel. In another instance, a woman on her way to a meeting in Chicago needed information on a particular industry as soon as she arrived. The library found the information and faxed it to her hotel so that she had it upon check-in. Service like that brings results—satisfied customers.

## RECOGNITION

Recognition comes in many forms. The quiet word-of-mouth referral to the library is just as satisfying as an award. But awards spread the news of your agency to more new business and validate your services. The library in Carroll County, Maryland (see chapter 7), received an award from the Public Library Association for their Lawyer Referral Service. The Newington, Connecticut, Library received a Special Recognition Award from the Chamber of Commerce for their efforts in assisting the business community.

The Town of Newington produces a Town/School/Business Collaborative newsletter that is mailed to each business and included with the library's business newsletter. In a recent issue, the Town Manager took it upon himself to trumpet the library's worth to the municipality (see Figure 8–1).

## FUNDING

Libraries involved in serving the business community recognize the importance of publicly acknowledging funds from sources outside the normal budgetary process. Announcements of grants and funding for everything from concert series to donated advertising appear in media ranging from local newspapers to billboards. Such publicity, in addition to strengthening the library's relationship with the donor, facilitates subsequent solicitations from other sources.

While the business reference staff generally has no direct role in the solicitation process, these individuals nevertheless do at times become involved. One business reference librarian was asked to elaborate on a children's program that a business had been asked to sponsor. The appropriate staff need to be aware of not only development activities but also the plans and programs going on within their own institutions.

The biggest funding impact of wider involvement in economic development can be an increase in the library's operating budget. Many libraries have clearly stated that without their economic development activities, their funding picture would be bleaker. The library's role in economic development often appears as a supporting argument for proposed funding levels at annual budget meetings. While it is too soon to measure the exact budgetary

**FIGURE 8-1    A Town Manager's Assessment of Newington's Public Library**

# TBSC

# Growth & Progress

A Publication of the Town Business School Collaborative                    September/October 1995

## Invaluable Economic Development Resource - The Public Library

*By Keith H. Chapman, Town Manager*

As Newington's Town Manager, I have realized the value of utilizing the public library in Newington's ongoing economic development efforts. The resources available at the Lucy Robbins Welles Library provide virtually instant results in researching existing companies for retention purposes and potential new companies in our recruitment efforts.

On numerous occasions the economic development staff or I have sought in depth information on a particular business that might be considering locating in our region. With the resources readily available at our library I can obtain a complete dossier of that company, including headquarters location, branch locations, number of employees, type of products or services provided, annual sales, members of the Board of Directors, CEO and other high level staff members names, addresses, phone numbers, and other pertinent data that not only assists the Town in understanding the needs of the company, but also serves as a foundation for a professional approach by the Town to that company.

The calling effort by library staff to existing businesses in Newington serves to achieve many objectives of the Town. A very positive image is presented in this calling effort by

our professional librarians. The information retrieved by the staff on these scheduled calls provides me with a constant assessment on the level of satisfaction of the CEO's

> *An introduction to business owners and key personnel of the library's services and resources can provide an immediate, positive impact which will be of lasting value.*

and company personnel in relation to the Town, region and State of Connecticut. The needs and desires of our business community can be conveyed and responded to quickly by the appropriate Town agencies.

The interaction of the library staff with our elected and appointed officials in regard to economic development is highly valued as well.

The magnitude of resource information the library has to offer our business sector has until recently gone unnoticed and underutilized. While we have found the library to be an integral part of our economic development team concept, Newington's library still is only one of a handful of libraries to realize this potential.

I have viewed the library as an integral part of our economic development effort and feel that a town that fails to tap this resource is not using its available resources to the maximum. The library is also available to our business sector. An introduction to business owners and key personnel of the library's services and resources can provide an immediate, positive impact which will be of lasting value.

## Pizzeria Uno Restaurant

Pizzeria Uno Restaurant Chicago Bar & Grill will occupy the 6,360 square foot pad site at Newington Commons. Pizzeria Uno is a full service restaurant. There are 136 Unos nationally, five in Connecticut. Nearby restaurants are at West Farms Mall and the Buckland Hills Mall in Manchester. Newington Commons Uno Restaurant will occupy the northwest corner of the site adjacent to the intersection of Kitts Lane and the Berlin Turnpike. This location will be visible to motorists using the Turnpike.

impact of economic development involvement on the actual libraries involved, the examples cited throughout this book all point to a higher regard for these institutions, which can lead to positive funding action.

## CONCLUSION

Entering the economic development arena involves understanding the total picture, retraining staff, and rethinking service delivery. But the slow, steady payback to the community can result in tangible growth for the businesses as well as residents who benefit from a vibrant economy. Library service that impacts the bottom line speaks directly to the funding bodies and policymakers in hard economic times. In order to continue to be a viable institution, libraries must seek out ways to impact the economy upon which they depend.

# APPENDIX A:
# THE BUSINESS PLAN

A document written to raise money for a growing company is known as a business plan. It is given to parties interested in investing in a business, be they a commercial bank or a venture capital source.

Creating a business plan may be the impetus behind a business person turning to the library for the first time. It is important that staff members working with businesses are familiar with the elements of the plan that library information can assist with.

The following are components of a business plan, with notations of useful library resources where applicable:

I.   Executive Summary
    — includes conclusions of each section of the plan in synopsis or narrative form

II.  Company Description
    — includes the mission statement; goals and objectives; name of the business; legal form (corporation, general or limited partnership); ownership; location; shareholders; board of directors and officers; stage of development; financial status (outstanding obligations); products and services; patents and licenses (secured or pending)

III. Industry Analysis
    — includes description of the industry of which the business is a part; current trends; opportunities that exist
        (Library resources: key ratio comparisons with other companies through *Almanac of Business and Industrial Financial Ratios*; *RMA Annual Statement Studies*; *U.S. Industrial Outlook*)

IV.  Target Market
    — includes who customers are, what they want, where they live, what they can afford
        (Library resources: *The Survey of Buying Power Data Service* [an expansion of the information published in *Sales and Marketing Magazine* each July and October]; *Sourcebook of Demographics & Buying Power for Every ZIP Code in the USA*)

V. The Competition
— who they are and the impact on your business; future competition

(Library resources: Business directories categorized by SIC code; local Chamber of Commerce directories; other locally produced directories; Yellow Pages)

VI. Marketing Plan and Sales Strategy
— how to promote and sell your business, service, or product; includes the compensation of the sales force.

(Library resources: *Personnel Management Services; Standard Rate and Data Services; Working Press of the Nation;* media guides; trade-show directories; telephone directories; motivational audio tapes and books)

VII. Operations
— how you run your business, including day-to-day functions suppliers; facilities issues; labor force; use of new technology; research and development plans; inventory control; supply and distribution

(Library resources: *What to Buy for Business; Buyer's Laboratory Reports; Thomas Register; Staffing a Small Business; Hiring, Compensation & Evaluating;* listings of consultants; state labor force statistics; local traffic studies; local utility costs)

VIII. Management and Organization
— people who will determine the success of the company; how they will be trained and used, and succession planning; management philosophy

(Library resources: books, tapes, and videos on management theories, style, and structure; books on personnel policies, rewards, and incentives; listings of consultants)

IX. Long-Term Development and Exit Plan
— what the company will look like in five and ten years; evaluating goals, milestones, risks; how the company will end (being acquired by a bigger company, becoming a franchise, going public, being handed down to the next generation, closing)

X. The Financials
— accounting methods; cash-flow analysis; sources and uses of funds

(Library resources: books on accounting methods; computer software to try out; forms and worksheets used in accounting practices)

Besides understanding the components of the plan and guiding the business person to good resources, the library can provide a computer with a laser-quality printer to write and print out the plan. There are even business plan templates available on disk to help the plan writer get started.

# APPENDIX B:
# ORGANIZING FOCUS GROUPS AT A REASONABLE COST

A focus group is a carefully planned discussion designed to obtain perceptions on a defined area of interest in a permissive, nonthreatening environment. It is conducted with approximately seven to ten people by a skilled interviewer. Marketing professionals customarily run focus groups in specially designed locations that are outfitted with one-way glass and comfortable seating that may simulate a living room. The cost of having a "classic" focus group is well beyond the realm of most libraries. In fact, calling in the professionals with all the "big city" trappings could have a negative impact on future library services, depending upon the sophistication of the community.

You don't need to be daunted by possible high costs; focus groups can be run without one-way glass rooms and expensive facilitators. A properly planned and executed comfortable discussion will directly benefit the participants and the library.

First, you need a clearly defined reason to have a focus group. No matter how economically you run it, the exercise demands time and energy and involves some risks. You should be on the brink of unveiling a product or service to the business community. If you are in touch with your business community through normal channels, your instincts are probably right and you'll be using the focus group for fine-tuning and building partnerships for your endeavor.

There are five requirements for focus groups to be successful: commitment, organization, good discussion leadership, participation, and follow-up.

## COMMITMENT

A focus group take time—before, during and after. The people who are organizing it and the administration have to buy into what the focus groups will be discussing and to implementing the suggestions they hear. If you're just going through the motions because focus groups are the "in" thing to do, the attitude will show and will discredit your efforts.

## ORGANIZATION

Someone—whether a paid staff member, a volunteer, or a consultant—must be responsible for managing the details of the focus group process. That person will need to:

1. Set the starting time and length based on the attendees. Early morning may work for people in the construction industry; later may be better for people dropping children off at day care; noon may be best for those accustomed to lunch time meetings. *Ninety minutes in length is the absolute maximum.* Time of day is one of the most critical decisions you will make. Try out your time on a few potential attendees before announcing it to avoid making the wrong choice.

2. Compile a list of invitees. How many groups are you going to run? You want to avoid redundant results, so resist the temptation to do ten groups when four will tell you what you want to know.

   You can divide the groups by industry: manufacturers, service providers, retailers, nonprofit organizations, and so on. You can divide them by status within the company: CEO, office manager, marketing specialist, human resources head, and the like. Or consider size of business to facilitate the best discussion. There is no one right way. Each has its merits.

3. Plan the logistics.

   • *Where will it be held?* While the library seems the most logical place, it may not be the place in which participants will be the most comfortable or that will offer the most convenience. Consider alternatives such as the meeting room at a local business, a conference room in your municipal building, or even a private room in a restaurant or coffee shop. The main idea at this point is that participants be comfortable.

- *Food is important.* Serving food is not a requirement, but it does help to break down barriers and encourage small talk. Providing the group with breakfast, lunch, or even dinner from a local caterer could be an opportune way to introduce a business service to potential business users. If you can't find a caterer to supply it free or at an affordable rate for your budget, a library staff member or volunteer will be busy cooking or purchasing and, definitely, cleaning up. You have to decide how you want to use the staff energy available to you.

- Another component of logistics is *the recording of the event.* Others will need to review what transpires in the sessions so that comparisons may be made among the groups. The options are an audio tape recorder, video recorder, and/or a person able to take copious notes.

Tape recorders work if they are centrally located and everyone speaks loudly. Video recorders work if they can be positioned to pick up everyone's body language and are unobtrusivc. A person to take full and useful notes has to have a grasp of the discussion so that the important points are recorded.

The ideal is a combination. Place a video recorder on a stand in the most central but out-of-the-way location possible. Have a tape recorder running farthest away from the video recorder, and have more than one person taking notes. That way, you'll catch at least a portion of the body language and most likely be able to record the conversation in total.

- If you are having the focus group at the library, be prepared to *offer a tour of library services* following the group. And also be prepared for no one to stay. Remember that they've already given up a part of their workday to benefit you (as they see it at this point), and any more time that you get from them is a bonus. But if you do have some takers, tell the person who is leading the tour to speak in terms of *benefits* to the business person, not *features.* For instance, don't say, "This is the new CD-ROM product, *American Business Disk*. It contains thousands of companies with all the information you might need." Instead say, "A company used the new *American Business Disk* just yesterday to find all the trucking companies in the state before sending out an invitation to bid." Keep the tour brief and hand out your business card to participants so they'll get back to you with questions.

4. Prepare the three or four questions you'll ask. Depending on the number of participants, you'll only have time for a couple of questions, so make sure the questions are the kind that elicit results, or everyone's time will be wasted. Questions that deal with the participants' perception of the library and its ability to deliver information to them are helpful.

5. Determine what you are going to do with the information you've gathered. Is there a task group ready to hear the results and formulate a plan? Has time been set aside to analyze the responses? The coordinator should be charged with guiding the entire process from beginning to end.

## DISCUSSION LEADERSHIP

Look for a person who understands the message you are trying to get across and the questions you want to ask. The person should be skilled at running discussions, be nonintrusive, and be able to keep the conversation flowing. That person could be the library administrator, a staff member, a library board member, or a volunteer from the community. The person should be fairly neutral and not well known to any of the participants. Most important, the discussion facilitator must understand that what is being said is to be treated confidentially. One solution would be to invite a librarian from a nearby community to serve as the facilitator in exchange for your reciprocal services.

The closer the library staff is to the process, the more they will buy into it. You can consider having a staff observer attend to take notes, to answer any questions that might arise or ask for clarification on any comments, and to offer a tour after. That person should not, however, be a participant in the discussion. Holding a separate focus group for staff to get their input, though, can be very informative.

## PARTICIPATION

This is the hardest part! Business people are very busy. As has been stated over and over, their time is their most precious commodity. So how do you get them to attend? First, send out a letter to all potential participants telling them the time, place, and what you want them to do. But don't expect that they'll remember the letter when you call to follow up. (And you will have to call—very few people RSVP on their own.) Then, use the same strategy you might use for a social gathering: Try peer pressure. Once you've snagged the most respected business person, call the next person and say, "George said he hoped he would see you there also."

You will need to invite almost twice as many as you want to come. Business people have busy lives and demanding schedules and last-minute emergencies are often the reason for nonattendance, not lack of interest. If your town is very small, consider going to a social gathering of a group of business people and inviting them face to face. Then follow it up with a phone call the next business day.

## FOLLOW-UP

Have thank-you notes addressed and ready to go as soon as the group concludes. A small gift of notecards, a canvas book bag, or a T-shirt with the library's logo is always appreciated. Then, if appropriate, put the participants on a special mailing list to receive updates on your progress. If any of them don't have library cards, send them one. Identify those who are your real advocates and promote that relationship. Call some of them to run ideas by. Form an ad hoc advisory group, if they are willing. Let them know what the conclusions of the groups were and your progress toward acting on suggestions. Ask them to return a year later to react to what you've done.

If you've done a good job, you've not only gathered new ideas and new perspectives but also turned observers into supporters for business library services. Some participants may be willing to give in-kind services to the library. One or two may become active in local government and remember what your goals are and how they might be funded.

# APPENDIX C:
# THE STRATEGIC PLAN OF
# THE GWINNETT-FORSYTH
# REGIONAL LIBRARY

The process of planning services to the business community must include the library board from the start. Providing business service represents a new direction, one that not all board members may be comfortable with until they totally understand the economic need for information. Some board members may be representatives of the very community for which you are trying to develop services, so—try out your ideas on members with whom you feel most comfortable; they could become your strongest advocates. And you may find you attract people within the business community to serve on the board—people who had formerly seen the library only as a place for children and leisure reading.

The Gwinnett-Forsyth Regional Library in Georgia used focus groups to develop a set of goals for serving the business community. These goals ultimately became part of a strategic business plan reviewed and approved by the library board. The document, reproduced below, provides a sound model of a statement of principles and approaches.

## SERVICES

The Business Information Center will enhance current services that can guarantee the Gwinnett and Forsyth business communities and individuals current information in a timely fashion and in the best format available to meet the needs of customers.

1. *Promote the services offered by the Business Center by visiting area businesses, speaking to business organizations, and participating in Chamber of Commerce tradeshows.* The Business Center's manager will aggressively seek opportunities to explain its services and to demonstrate what the Center can do for businesses. This

strategy is the best way to promote the Center's capabilities.

2. *Provide tours and training sessions in the use of business databases on an individual or group basis.* Center staff will incorporate innovative training techniques such as developing training videos on searching business databases. Demonstrations of the System's databases will be provided by Center staff as part of their regular work schedule.

3. *Develop a close partnership with the Gwinnett and Forsyth Chambers of Commerce to provide mutually beneficial programs and services.* The Business Center will assist the Chambers in providing needed information to area businesses in order to ensure the continued economic development of Gwinnett and Forsyth counties.

4. *Implement a fax policy that permits the faxing of information when permissible by the Copyright Law.* This service provides greater convenience for businesses or individuals when immediate access to information is essential.

5. *Work with county and municipal governments to provide area businesses with needed local information.* The Library System and the Gwinnett County government are currently exploring the feasibility of making certain county records (i.e., business licenses, county tax records, county procurement, planning and development information) available through the library's online catalog. Serving as an access point for this type of information would be a tremendous help to area businesses.

6. *Provide convenient access to business information.* The Library System will develop strategies to provide easy access to information. Such strategies might include: (1) dial-in service to business databases. The System will continue to be an advocate for dial-in access to databases when negotiating licensing agreements with database vendors; (2) gathering and packaging information for businesses in the best format available; the Business Center will gather information and distribute requested information in a timely fashion; (3) a more centralized location for the Business Center; (4) circulating business materials will be distributed throughout the System based on demand.

## COLLECTION DEVELOPMENT

The Business Information Center will maintain a reference collection that is as current as possible and the library system will provide current circulating material in the best formats available.

1. *Emphasis will be placed on maintaining a broad, general reference collection with particular interest being given to metro-Atlanta and Georgia directories, periodicals, and other business sources.* Patron requests and the Business Center Focus Group indicate that local information is of primary interest. The Business Center will actively pursue a partnership with the local communities to obtain this hard to find information.

2. *Circulating materials will be purchased in the subject areas of small business development, investments, importing and exporting, product development, management, and high technology.* The Business Center Manager will request that materials management target a percentage of the current circulating budget for business materials and will work with materials management in identifying quality materials in the most convenient formats.

3. *Apply for available grants to help support expanded services and specialized reference collections.*

## COMMUNITY INVOLVEMENT

Supplemental funding sources will be sought to provide the additional monies needed for the new reference services and expanded reference and circulating collections.

1. *Seek business sponsorships for database resources, periodical subscriptions, other business reference sources, and circulating business materials.* The Business Center will identify sources that have been requested but not purchased due to budgetary constraints (i.e., new materials that the Center has never had before, providing access to materials that would be helpful to other businesses, donate resources that would help us provide other services not currently offered).

# APPENDIX D:
# GUIDELINES FOR MEDICAL, LEGAL, AND BUSINESS RESPONSES AT GENERAL REFERENCE DESKS

## 1.0 INTRODUCTION

Library users need information in order to make decisions. They have a right to gain access to any published information available in library collections. Staff are responsible for providing complete and accurate responses to users' questions when possible and for guiding patrons to the most appropriate resources for their needs. (The terms "user" and "patron" are used interchangeably in this document.)

The following guidelines are designed to assist staff at general reference desks in meeting user needs and in responding to users requesting medical, legal, or business information. To ensure that malpractice claims will not follow, librarians need to keep current in their subject areas, refer questions beyond their level of competency to others, document search strategies and sources, and explain to the user the librarians' responsibility to provide sources rather than interpretation. Although these guidelines are written for medical, legal, and business reference service, they may be applied to any reference transaction.

Each library's reference collection should contain current, accurate, and accessible medical, legal, and business information appropriate to the needs of the community served. The reference transaction should fully satisfy the user's need for information, either by providing accurate sources in hand, or clear and concise referrals to obtainable sources located elsewhere.

Prepared by the Standards and Guidelines Committee, Reference and Adult Services Division, American Library Association. Reviewed and approved by the ALA Standards Committee, and adopted by the RASD Board of Directors, January 1992.

# 2.0 ROLE OF LIBRARIANS

When asked legal, medical, or business reference questions, librarians should make clear their role as information providers. Librarians can provide information but should not interpret that information. They should provide instruction in the use of resources, enabling users to pursue information independently and effectively, if so desired. Libraries should develop written disclaimers stating a position on providing specialized reference service.

## 2.1 INTERPRETATION

The reference librarian provides the library user with information but does not evaluate that information. If the patron has trouble understanding the source, an alternative source should be sought. If no appropriate sources can be located, the patron should be referred to the legal, medical, or financial community for interpretation of the information.

## 2.2 ADVICE

Libraries may advise patrons regarding the relative merits of sources and make recommendations regarding library materials when appropriate. Materials recommended should be the most comprehensive and the most current available.

## 2.3 CONFIDENTIALITY

Confidentiality of user requests must be respected at all times. Questions should not be discussed outside the library, and names should never be mentioned without the user's permission.

## 2.4 TACT

As in all situations, reference librarians should use discretion when interviewing users regarding medical, legal, and business questions. While it is important to conduct a thorough reference interview, this should be done in such a way as to minimize discomfort to the user. The librarian should try to identify the issue in question without intruding on the user's privacy. Librarians should be impartial and nonjudgmental in handling users' queries.

# 3.0 SOURCES

The library should acquire appropriate materials in medical, legal, and business subject areas that meet the needs of the community served. The reference librarian should direct the user to possible sources, both in and out of the library, where the information the user requires will be provided. These materials might include books, pamphlets, journals, electronic services, service agencies, and professionals in the appropriate field. When helping a user, librarians must be careful to avoid using technical terms. Under no circumstances should information be withheld from a user.

## 3.1 CURRENCY OF SOURCES

The reference librarian should always point out publication dates to the user. Because information in medical, legal, and business areas changes rapidly, the user should be advised that there may be more current information on the topic.

In subject areas where up-to-date information is essential, libraries should provide the most current information possible, consistent with the needs of the library's primary clientele and within the limitations of the library's materials budget and collection development policy.

Reference collections should be weeded periodically to remove dated materials in subject areas where up-to-date information is essential. If retention of older materials is required for historical purposes, distinctions in dates should be obvious.

## 3.2 REFERRALS TO OTHER SOURCES

Referrals should be made only if the librarian expects that the agency, service, individual, or other source can and will provide the information needed. Librarians should be prepared to refer questions to human as well as to written sources. Awareness of community, state, and private services outside of the library proper is important. Reference librarians may provide access to biographical and other information that is available in directories and other sources. They may not make recommendations to specific lawyers, legal firms, doctors, other medical care providers, or financial professionals. Users should be referred to county or state professional associations for additional information.

## 4.0 TELEPHONE OR MAIL REFERENCE

Special care must be taken with telephone, mail, electronic mail, and telefacsimile since it is easy to misinterpret phone messages, and written communications may need explanations or interpretation. Only factual information—such as dates, names and addresses, specific citations, or catalog checks—should be given out over the telephone. Brief information may be read verbatim without interpretation. The source should be given for all information provided. Users must come to the library, or be directed to a special library, for statutory or case law material, medical information beyond quoted definitions of terms from standard medical dictionaries, or financial information encompassing more than the above.

Telephone or mail requestors may have to be informed that the library does have information on the topic but that they will have to come into the library to use the material. Questions received through the mail should be answered with full citations for the source or with well-documented photocopies if such copies can be done within copyright requirements.

## 5.0 ETHICS

The American Library Association's current Code of Ethics (as stated in the ALA Policy Manual in the ALA Handbook of Organization) governs the conduct of all staff members providing information service.

# APPENDIX E: GLOSSARY

## COMMON BUSINESS TERMS TO KNOW

*Accounts payable*—a current liability representing the amount owed by an individual or a business to a creditor for merchandise or services purchased on an open account or short-term credit.

*Accounts receivable*—money owed a business enterprise for merchandise bought on open account.

*Amortize*—(1) to discharge a debt in periodic payments until the total, including the interest, has been paid; (2) to write off a portion or all of the cost of an asset; to retire debt over a period of time.

*Annuity*—(1) a series of equal payments at fixed intervals; (2) a scheduled payment to a retired person, synonymous with pension plan.

*Capital*—the amount invested in a venture.

*Cash flow*—the movement of money into and out of a company; actual income received and actual payments made out.

*DBA (Doing Business As)*—a company's trade name rather than the name by which it is legally incorporated.

*Direct mail list*—names and addresses of potential customers, purchased by or given without charge to an organization.

*Direct marketing*—(1) a marketing strategy in which the advertising message may be delivered by a variety of media rather than through the mail; (2) the activity of selling to consumers or industrial users without the use of the middle person.

*Due diligence*—the process undertaken by venture capitalists, investment bankers, or others to thoroughly investigate a company before financing it.

*Jobber*—a middleperson who handles merchandise in odd or job lots.

Sources: Jerry M. Rosenberg, *Dictionary of Business Management* (New York: Wiley, 1993); Rhonda M. Abrams, *The Successful Business Plan*, (Grants Pass, OR: Oasis Press, 1993).

*Job description*—a statement, usually in writing, of the responsibilities, approaches, conditions, and other relevant factors built into a job.

*Just in case manufacturing*—keeping inventory stocked in sufficient quantity to fill the customer's immediate need.

*Just in time manufacturing*—keeping inventory stocked only to the levels needed to produce goods just in time for delivery.

*Kaizen*—Japanese term for "continuous improvement."

*Lead time*—the elapsed time between the beginning of an economic or manufacturing function and the completion of that function.

*Leveraging*—the advantage (or disadvantage) obtained from using borrowed money to finance a business when the net interest rate of the borrowed funds is less (more) than the company's earnings.

*Limited partner*—A member of a partnership who is not personally liable for incurred debts of the partnership. By law, at least one partner must be fully liable.

*Line of credit*—an agreement between a bank and a customer whereby the bank agrees to lend the customer funds over a future period, up to an agreed maximum amount.

*Liquid*—capable of being readily converted to cash.

*Manufacturer's representative*—an independent sales agent for a group of manufacturers in a described sales territory.

*Market research*—the part of marketing research that deals with the pattern of a market, measuring the extent and nature of the market and identifying its characteristics.

*Market share*—the percentage of the total available customer base captured by a company.

*Marketing*—activities that accelerate the movement of goods or services from the manufacturer to the consumer.

*OSHA*—the Occupational Safety and Health Act of 1970.

*Partnership*—a contractual relationship between two or more people in a joint enterprise who agree to share, not necessarily equally, in the profits and losses of the organization.

*Patent*—a right, assigned for seventeen years to the inventor of a device or process, to exclude others from making, using, or selling the invention without permission.

*Point-of-sale terminal*—a communication and data-capture terminal located where payment is made for goods or services.

*POP (Point of purchase) advertising*—promotional material placed at the point of purchase, such as interior displays, printed materials at store counters, or window displays.

*Portfolio*—holdings of securities by an individual or institution.

*Price-earnings (p/e) ratio*—the price of a share of stock divided by earnings per share for a twelve-month period.

*Profit margin*—the amount of money earned after the cost of goods or all operating expenses are deducted.

*ROI*—return on investment; the amount earned in direct proportion to the capital invested.

*SEC*—the Securities and Exchange Commission, established by Congress to protect investors.

*Segmentation research*—a form of marketing research that uncovers new bases for market segmentation.

*SIC*—see Standard Industrial Classification.

*Spot advertising*—a campaign wherein advertisers choose specific stations to be used.

*Standard Industrial Classification System (SIC)*—a numerical system developed by the U.S. Bureau of the Budget to classify establishments by type of activity for purposes of facilitating the collection, tabulation, presentation, and analysis of data relating to such establishments and for promoting uniformity with U.S. agencies.

*Subcontracting*—work given out to another employer.

*10-K*—the financial report that is filed annually with the SEC by firms with securities traded on a national exchange or in the over-the-counter market.

*10-Q*—a quarterly report filed with the SEC that is usually unaudited.

*Trade name*—the name under which an organization conducts business or by which the business or its goods and services are identified. It may or may not be registered as a trademark.

*Turnkey*—a contractual agreement between a customer and an organization to provide full services or a complete product.

*Uniform Commercial Code (UCC)*—a set of statutes purporting to provide some consistency among states' commercial laws.

*Value added*—the part of the value of produced goods that is developed by the company.

*Venture capital*—funds invested in enterprises that do not usually have access to conventional sources of capital (such as banks, the stock market).

*Working capital*—the cash available to the company for the ongoing operations of the business.

# BIBLIOGRAPHY

Baker, Sharon L. "Improving Business Services Through the Use of Focus Groups." *RQ* (Spring 1991): 377–385.

Blakely, Edward J. *Planning Local Economic Development: Theory and Practice.* 2d ed. Thousand Oaks, CA: SAGE, 1994.

Bleiweis, Maxine. "Business Information Services with a Smile." *Marketing Treasures* (May/June 1995): 5–6.

*Business Networking Made Easy.* Video cassette. Produced by Prescott Group, distributed by 411 Video Information, 1994. 20 min.

Coffman, Steve, and Helen Josephine. "Doing It for Money." *Library Journal*, October 15, 1991: 32–36.

Committee for Economic Development. *Research and Policy Committee. Leadership for Dynamic State Economics.* New York: Committee for Economic Development, 1986.

————. *Restoring Prosperity: Budget Choices for Economic Growth: A Statement by the Research and Policy Committee for the Committee for Economic Development.* New York: Committee for Economic Development, 1992.

Covey, Stephen R. *The Seven Habits of Highly Effective People.* New York: Simon & Schuster, 1989.

Daniells, Lorna M. *Business Information Sources.* 3rd ed. Berkeley: University of California Press, 1993.

Durrance, Joan C. *Meeting Community Needs with Job and Career Services.* New York: Neal-Schuman, 1994.

Ellis, Brinille Eliane. "Strategic Economic Development." *MIS Report.* 26 (2) (February 1994).

Fleming, Helen Ruth. "Library CPR: Savvy Marketing Can Save Your Library." *Library Journal*, September 15, 1993: 32–35.

Freed, Melvyn N. and Virgil Diodato. *Business Information Desk Reference: Where to Find Answers to Business Questions.* New York: Macmillan, 1991.

Gray, John. *Men Are from Mars, Women Are from Venus: A Practical Guide for Improving Communication and Getting What You Want in Your Relationships.* New York: HarperCollins, 1993.

Illinois State Library, Special Reports Series. *Library Partners.* 2 (1) (1995).

Kober, Shirlee-Ann, and Maxine Bleiweis. "What do they want? Ask them!" *Connecticut Libraries* 34 (11) (December 1992): 1, 7, 8.

Krueger, Richard A. *Focus Groups: A Practical Guide for Applied Research.* 2d ed. Thousand Oaks, CA: SAGE, 1994.

Lavin, Michael R. *Business Information: How to Find It, How to Use It.* Phoenix: Oryx Press, 1992.

Miele, Tony, and Nancy Welch. "Libraries as Information Centers for Economic Development." *Public Libraries* (January/February 1995): 18–22.

Muir, Robert F. "Marketing Your Library or Information Service to Business." *Online* (July 1993): 41–46.

Osborne, David. "Keynote Speech: The Role of Information in the Economy of the Southeast." *The Southeastern Librarian* (Summer 1990): 57–59.

Pare, Terence P. "How to Find Out What They Want." *Fortune* 128 (Autumn/Winter 1993): 39–41.

Peete, Gary R. *Business Resources on the Internet PLUS: A Hands-On Workshop.* San Carlos, California: Library Solutions Press, 1995.

"Playing by New Rules: Nine Economic Development Realities for the 90's." Washington, DC: Corporation for Enterprise Development, 1990.

Riechel, Rosemarie. *Public Library Services to Business.* New York: Neal-Schuman, 1994.

Ruetenik, Lynne S. "A Lament: Do We Miss the Good Life!" *Hartford Courant*, March 5, 1995, C:1.

Rusk, David. *Cities Without Suburbs.* 2nd ed. Baltimore, Maryland: Johns Hopkins University Press, 1995.

Schlessinger, Bernard and Rachel S. Karp. *The Basic Business Library: Core Resources.* 3rd ed. Phoenix: Oryx Press, 1995.

Tannen, Deborah. *You Just Don't Understand: Women and Men in Conversation.* New York: William Morrow, 1990.

Wilson, W. Randall. "Partners in Economic Development." *Library Journal* March 15, 1986: 32–34.

Woy, Pat. "In-house Market Research." *Home Office Computing* (June 1994): 32–34.

# INDEX

# COLOPHON

Maxine Bleiweis is the Library Director for the public library in Newington, Connecticut. She is past president of the Connecticut Library Association. She received her MLS from Rutgers University. She has spoken at national, regional, and local conferences on the public library's role in providing service to the business sector.